Early
American
Advertising

Early American Advertising

Compiled by Bob Perlongo

ART DIRECTION BOOK COMPANY

New York, N.Y. 10016

for Ingrid with love

Library of Congress Catalog Card Number: 84-071519
ISBN: 0-88108-015-2

Printed in the United States of America

Published by ART DIRECTION BOOK COMPANY
10 East 39th Street
New York, New York 10016

Contents

It all began in Babylon, or so they say. Hired barkers hawking wares in the street, shouters from wickety wagons laden with goods both licit and ill, signs above shops showing the symbols of the varied trades: of such legendary yet ultimately pedestrian stuff are made the roots of advertising.

The ancient Greeks and Egyptians, as one might imagine, had a large hand in shaping early oral ad art. Generations of their hired criers heralded the arrival of ships and the sale of the seaborne cargoes. These were the forerunners of the industrious Yankee Pedlars of colonial days, the tinsmiths and scissors grinders, the hangers out of shingles all along the Atlantic and later across the land.

For a long old time, when only those with vested interests and a very few adventuresome others could read, the spoken blurb and the painted sign prevailed together in graphic ad-dom: the medium was definitely not yet the message. Only very gradually would the advertising *word*, as such, make its way, and then it would do so with a vengeance, doing unto language whatever had to be done to do the selling—"Like a cigarette should."

It was in the nineteenth century, and mainly in America, that ad word and ad symbol blossomed together. It was the era of novelty and bombast, the heyday of Phineas Barnum and all that gaudy ilk—and a time when woodcuts and copperplate engravings were *the* media for visual selling. Fragile or bold, busy or simple, they did well the job of

the long-ago hawker who tugged at Babylonian sleeves: they played
their part with style and grace and a timeless rustic charm.

Soon would come the photograph and the halftone drawing—the
shiny new wonders of gravure—to usurp most of the woodcut-carver's
and engraver's role. Their patient artistry would now be adjudged
economically infeasible for newspapers and magazines; book illustration
would be their new, narrower dominion. And although theirs was the
end of an advertising era, they are far from forgotten, as will attest many
ad art lovers and socio-history buffs who today are waxing increasingly
avid over old-time ad lore. Nostalgia is the journey that gets us there,
back to that magical time when everything was better even if it wasn't,
back when they wrote those great old ads they don't write anymore.

* * *

*(Note: Publication dates of the ads are given, where known. Undated
ads are all from the same general period, late nineteenth- to early
twentieth-century. Remember, since these ads are that old, the addresses
and offers listed therein are no longer valid—so save your postage.)*

I A gallery of advertisements and commentaries

(1815)

The first print-media made especially for advertising were simple affairs indeed: boats, animals, articles of home and market—clear-cut eye-catchers that were only incidentally "quaint." The eagle being the national bird, it was quite natural for it to fly high among the favored birds of commerce. One saw them pushing any number of people and things, from politicians to printing ink, as in the ad above and the one on the facing page.

MASSACHUSETTS, all hail.

ELECTORS—Remember OLD FRIENDS,—and take —ONCE MORE, " *the Long Pull, the STRONG pull, and the pull alltogether;*" to strengthen their hands, and convince the world that the Citizens of a Republic are not always ungrateful.

STATE *NOMINATIONS.*

HIS EXCELLENCY

CALEB STRONG, Esq.

FOR GOVERNOR.

HIS HONOR.

WILLIAM PHILLIPS, Esq.

FOR LT.-GOVERNOR.

SENATORIAL NOMINATIONS.

MIDDLESEX,
Hon. John Brooks,
Calvin Sanger, Esq.
Samuel P. P. Fay, Esq.
NORFOLK,
Joseph Heath, Esq.
James Richardson, Esq.
BERKSHIRE,
Hon. Joseph Whiton,
Wolcott Hubbell, Esq.
BARNSTABLE,
Hon. Wendall Davis.

CUMBERLAND,
Hon. Lathrop Lewis,
Hon. Jacob Abbot.
KENNEBEC,
Samuel Reddington, Esq.
OXFORD,
Hon. Daniel Stowell.
YORK,
Joseph Dane, Esq.
Abiel Hall, Esq.
LINCOLN, &c.
Benjamin Hasey, Esq.
William Crosby, Esq.
Ebenezer Inglee, Esq.

(1852)

By the mid-1800s, shipping posters developed along the lines of a definite, easily recognized format: the destination appeared at the top of the ad above the engraving of the vessel, and the vessel's name and other details were listed below.

FOR
CHAGRES & SAN JUAN.
THE FIRST-CLASS STEAMSHIP

OSPRAY
Captain L. R. Westfall,
Will Sail for the above named Ports.
On Thursday, March 25, 1852.
NO BERTHS SECURED UNTIL PAID FOR.
For Freight or Passage apply to
GEO. E. HAMILTON, Agent,
Over the Ocean Bank, corner of Greenwich & Fulton Sts.
NEW-YORK.

(1852)

Gentlemen's Clothing,

FURNISHING GOODS, &c.

The popular and unrivalled low priced Clothing House, known as Oak Hall, has now stood the test for thirteen years & public opinion has resolved that the course adopted by the proprietor to supply the multitude with good apparel at a very small advance upon the cost of the materials and labor, is the surest plan to secure the general patronage; therefore his first and original motto of LARGE sales and SMALL PROFITS he is fully satisfied is the only true and sure course, and he is resolved to pursue it. He is now prepared with his enormous Stock of Ready Made Garments, of every fabric style and finish, for the farmer, or the laboring man,— the gentleman of fashion or mechanic; and who will be here after provided for sale to the public at LOWER PRICES than ever before known, even at this very large and low priced House, Clergy, Clerks, Youths, Business Men, Salaried Men, Military Officers and men, and all others wishing to avoid full one third of the total cost of the season's Clothing should bear in mind it can be done at Simmons's W. Simmons's highly popular Clothing House, where Youths' & Gents' Apparel may be procured at a saving of more than thirty per centum. This is a FIXED FACT; & all who come to buy can be ensured of the correctness of this position. Call at SIMMONS'S OAK HALL.

Youths' and Little Children's CLOTHING, of all sizes and every variety,

AT EXTREMELY LOW PRICES.

Oak Hall,

Gothic Front, Diamond Windows,

34 North Street

(1850)

Above, a prime example of how typeset matter and graphic elements were sometimes merged. The "Oak Hall" words-in-letters message didn't really need to be intelligible, but it was a nice bonus for those readers intrigued enough to want to wend their way through the letters to see what in the Sam Hill this Oak Hall was all about.

GET THE BEST.

THOMSON'S

PATENT GLOVE FITTING AND

CROWN CORSETS!

The Patent GLOVE FITTING CORSETS are unrivalled in the United States, Canada, and throughout the whole of Europe.

THEY RECEIVED THE HIGHEST AWARD at WORLD'S FAIR, London, the PARIS EXPOSITION, the PHILADELPHIA, and the AMERICAN INSTITUTE FAIR.

This cut is a correct representation of our D. Quality Corset.

The following is a copy of the Judges' Report at the Semi-Centennial Exhibition of the American Institute Fair, 1881:—

No. 1,161, Corsets, Thomson, Langdon & Co., 70 and 72 Worth Street, New York City.— These corsets are superior to any others on exhibition. We recommend them for shape, style, quality of material, finish and general excellence, and worthy of all merit as claimed for them by the manufacturers. We recommend the Medal of SUPERIORITY.

The above award for SUPERIORITY was the HIGHEST and ONLY ONE OF THE KIND made at the Fair.

In addition to rights secured by patents, the Trade-Mark, Names and Representations of these Corsets are secured by copyright to guard the Public against inferior and imitation goods.

See that the name THOMSON and the Trade-Mark A CROWN,—are stamped on every pair. NO OTHER IS GENUINE.

TRADE MARK

THOMSON, LANGDON & CO.,

70 & 72 Worth Street, New York, Sole Manufacturers.

(1882)

Promises, promises were — and, for that matter, still are — the advertiser's stock-in-trade. Here the promise is in the picture, with accompanying copy of unusual restraint. These quiet, pithy boasts exude a sense of self-confident dignity, as befitting an established purveyor of discreet clothing.

THOMSON'S NEW STYLES
IMPROVED GLOVE-FITTING

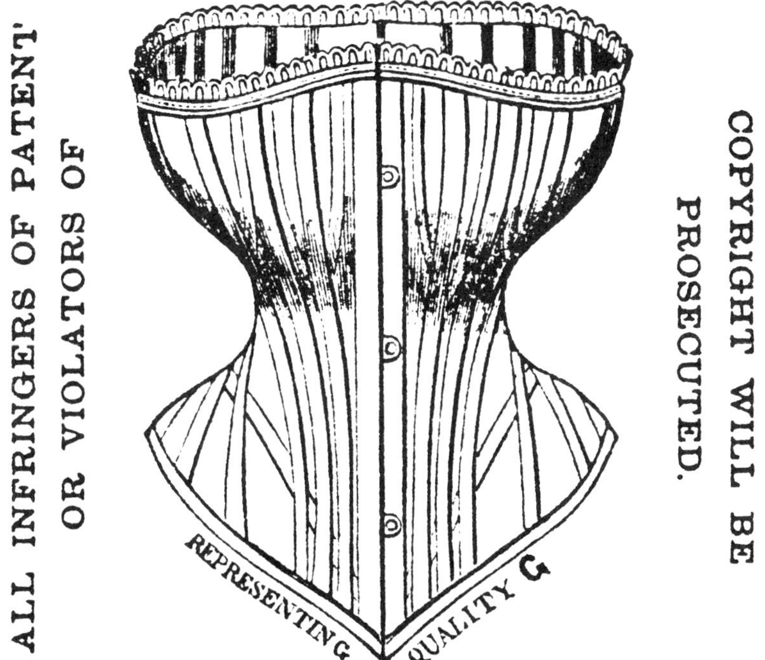

The **GLOVE-FITTING CORSET**, as now produced in its **IMPROVED** SHAPE, FULLNESS OF BUST, and LENGTH, is pronounced FAULTLESS.

It is the **Most Popular Corset** ever introduced into the American Market.

THOMSON, LANGDON & CO. Patentees,

391 BROADWAY, N. Y.

(1871)

The appeal to vanity has always been a formidable factor in the art of advertising. In the ad above and the one at the right the promise of ideal shapeliness is the key the manufacturers hope will unlock milady's secret heart — and purse. As Alphonse Karr so aptly put it (in 1849): *"Plus ça change, plus c'est même chose."* ("The more things change, the more they are the same.")

COX & PURVES,
MANUFACTURERS OF
ZEPHYR BOSOM PADS.
(Patented January 27th, 1874.)
THE ONLY INFLATING PADS,
Concave and Ventilating.
Sample Pads Mailed on Receipt of Price,
$1.00.
SPECIAL TERMS TO JOBBERS.
Office and Factory, 355 W. 10th st., N. Y.

(1874)

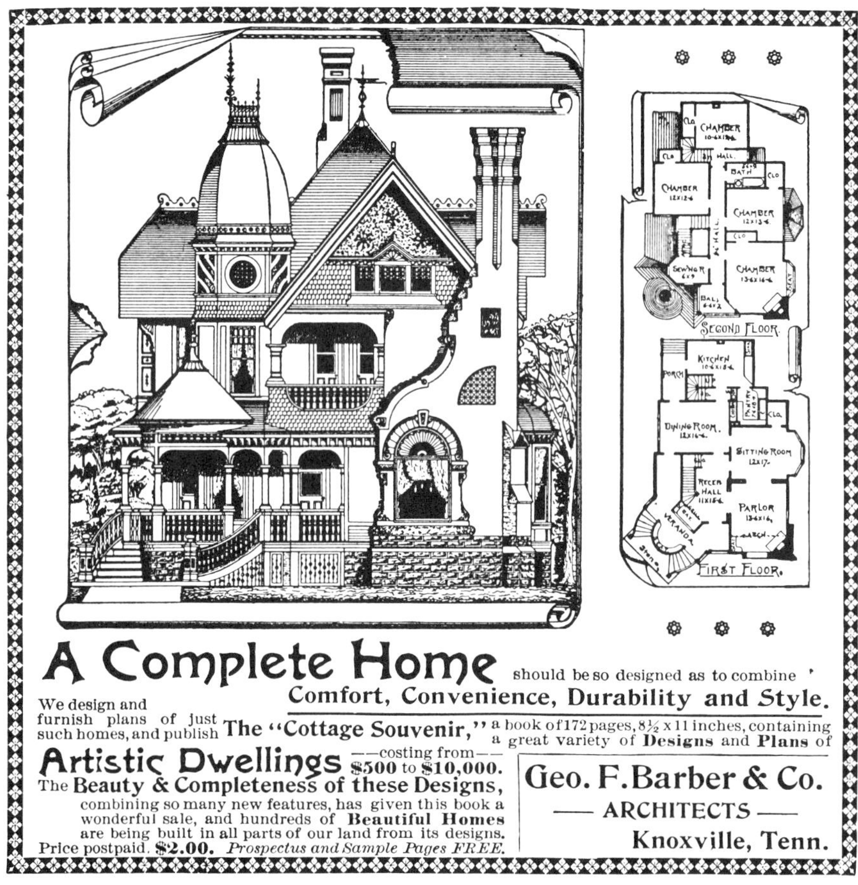

For $2.00, a reader of this 1892 advertisement could obtain (postpaid) a 172-page book of "Designs and Plans of Artistic Dwellings." For the skeptical, these architects made a little offer they hoped could not be refused: "Prospectus and Sample Pages FREE."

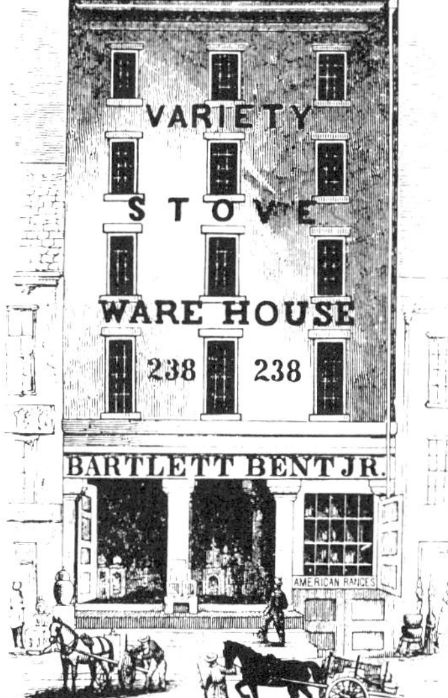

There were times, in old-time ad-dom, when dabbling with type got out of hand — as it threatens to here. Were it not for the strongly positioned linecut and the carefully balanced overall layout, the great variety of typefaces used in this ad might easily have been self-defeating.

LORD & TAYLOR,

Importers and Wholesale and Retail Dealers in

DRY GOODS.

Nos. 255, 257, 259 & 261 Grand Street, cor. Chrystie, N. Y.

This boldly dignified Lord & Taylor ad appeared in 1854, and it did its part to help set the tone of the company's advertising efforts for more than a century — demonstrating the durability of an image when backed by continuing public acceptance in the marketplace.

12

A strictly logical mind might balk at this copy's swift transition from a horse's harness dressing to the acceptance of a young man's proposal of marriage (to his ''sweet-heart,'' not his horse). But strict logic isn't often what sells, and besides, one is rather compelled by the fervor of belief embodied in the parting-shot pronouncement: ''Any young man who has his future at stake should be sure to have his harness thoroughly dressed with this dressing before he takes his best girl to ride.''

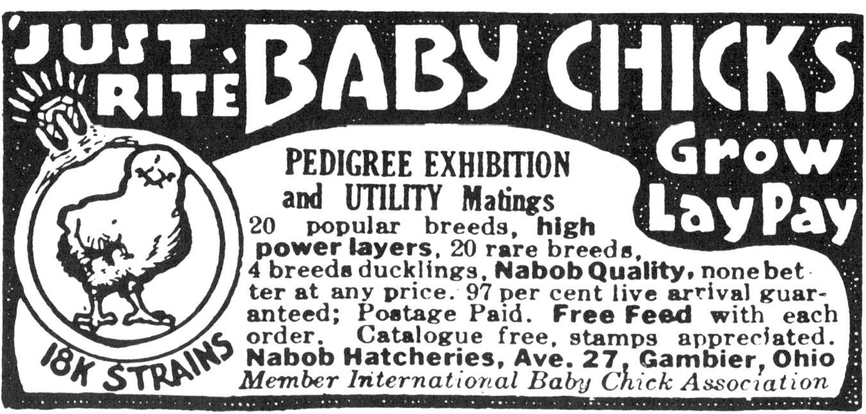

Two samples of the rustic approach to nineteenth-century print-media selling. Illustrations such as the above were in their heyday then, as more and more advertisers began to rely on them to catch the reader's passing gaze.

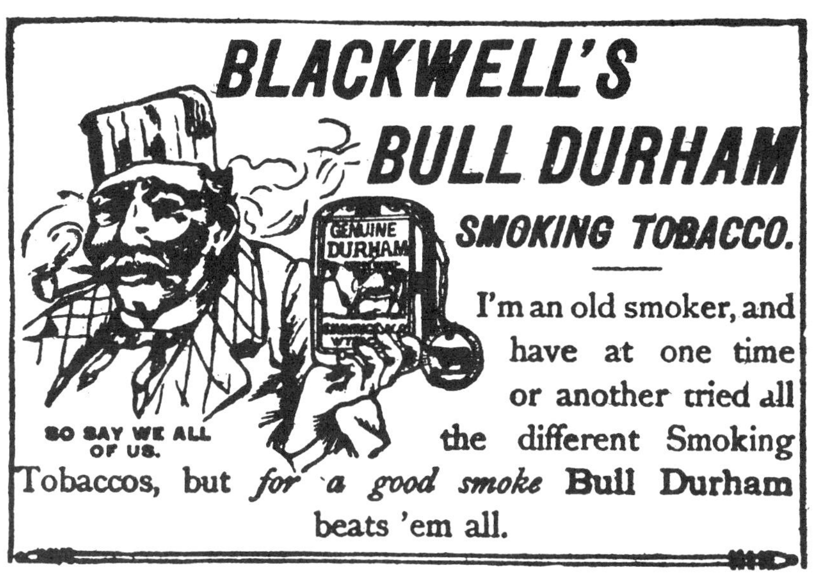

Super-straight and simple is the message here, in as calm and collected a testimonial-type ad as you're likely to find, whatever the era. And effective such advertising must have been, since the advertiser — venerable old Bull Durham — is still very much in business, rolling down the years.

SORE NIPPLES.—Dr A. C. CASTLE, 297 Broadway, says he has known Sherman's Papillary Oil cure the worst cases in a short time, where every thing else failed.

The Hon. B B. Beardsley's lady suffered for six weeks with sore nipples; her physician tried every thing his skill could devise : she thought she should lose them when a friend recommended Sherman's Papillary Oil ; she tried it and was immediately relieved, and perfectly cured in five days. This invaluable article is for sale at 106 Nassau street, 643 Broadway, New York, and at 139 Fulton strc c Broeklyn,   n18

Medical advertising, circa the Gay Nineties. It was an era of scant regulation, and the range in ad quality — and credibility — was broad indeed. The above specimen is typical of countless similarly pseudo-dignified announcements that promised amazing cures for ills of every imaginable sort. On the other hand, there *were* reputable advertisers, such as Lydia Pinkham, whose puffery was well within the bounds of decorum. Note that then, as now, endorsements abounded. Ready or not, the dawning of the age of the Satisfied Customer (or Prescriber, as the case may be) was upon us.

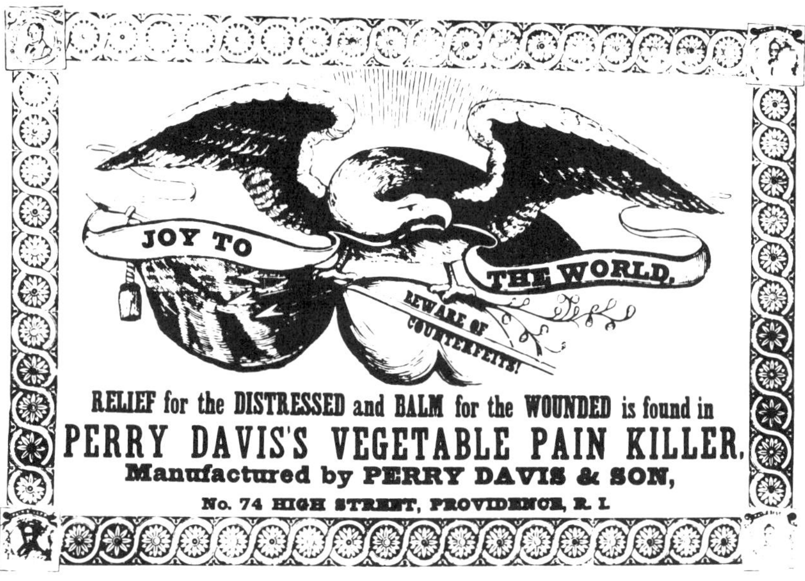

The legacy of countless witch doctors and patent-medicine pitchmen — lightfooted spookers down the ages — can be seen clearly in these old-time "medical" ads, typical of a whole subspecies of ad art which flourished throughout the 1800s by making the most extravagant claims for their lotions and potions and guaranteed (and largely bogus) cure-alls. Here we are offered a pain-killer for the "distressed" and "wounded" (heralded by our omnipresent advertising eagle) and — most remarkable of all — a fill-it-yourself home dentistry kit!

Sometimes, there seemed to be nothing the wonder wares of the medical ads couldn't cure, including ''cancer and scrofula.'' Quite amazingly, yet in matter-of-fact fashion, the fine print at the bottom of the lady's scroll claims that Acme Hair Dye ''will curl straight hair, and straighten curled hair.''

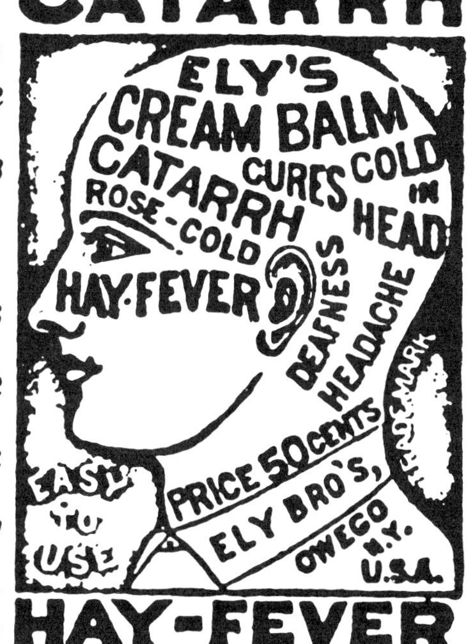

Content aside, many medical ads were distinguished purely as pieces of graphic artistry, as witness this pre-Pop-Artish number for Ely's Cream Balm. Brand recognition was accomplished quite effectively by use of that incredible, and readily identifiable, lettered head.

Real estate advertising, 1801 style. The look was simple-to-crude, the pitch stoutly straightforward. Note the now-freaky-seeming forms "dwellinghoufe" and "fituation."

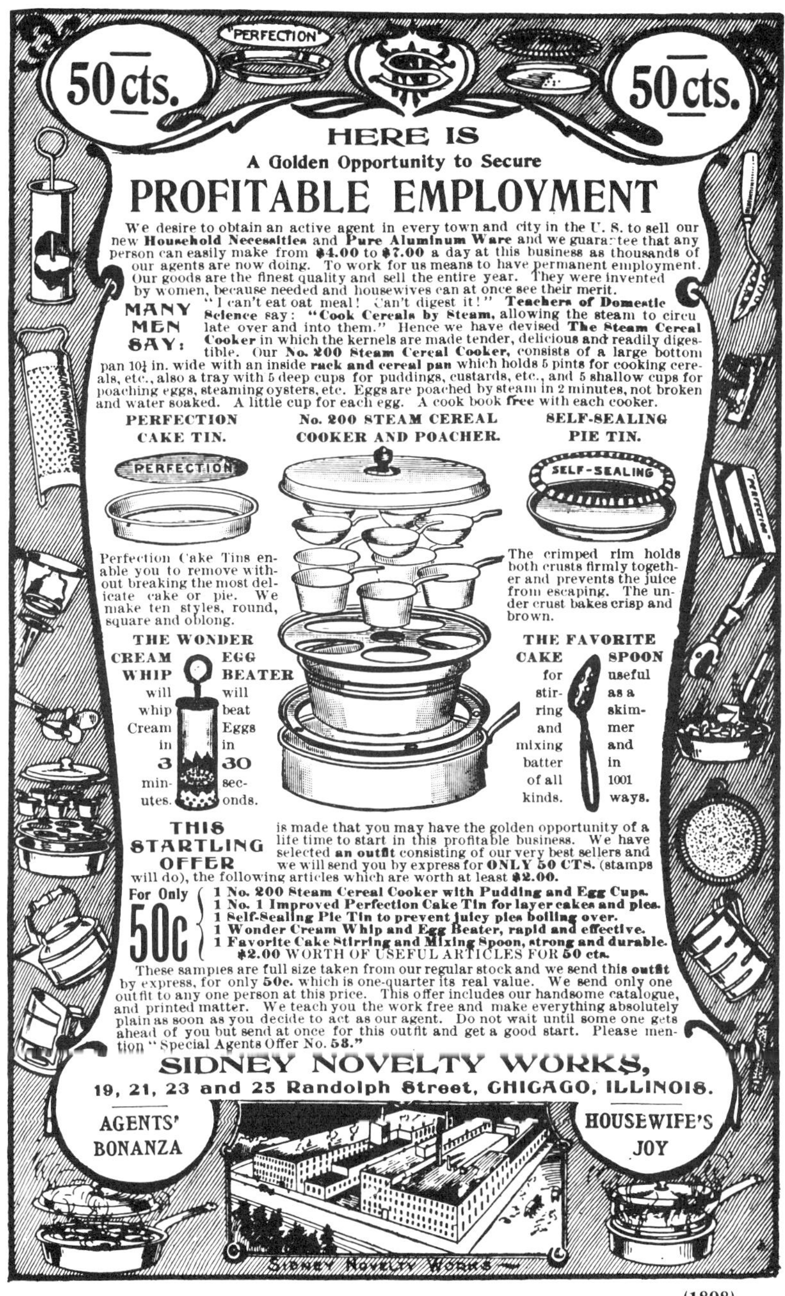

(1898)

Selling would-be sellers was (and is) the name of the sell-it-yourself, free-lance employment game. Here the means to the rainbow's end is a miscellaneous armada of "Household Necessities and Pure Aluminum Ware" — "only one outfit to any one person at this price." The price? All of 50¢.

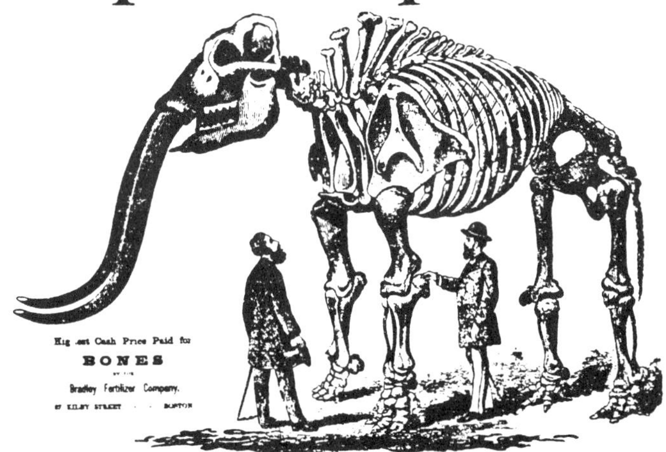

(1887)

Bones are the business in this attention-grabbing poster put out by the Bradley fertilizer people. The inspired device of the mastodon's skeleton does graphic wonders for a subject not inherently very thrilling to the layman.

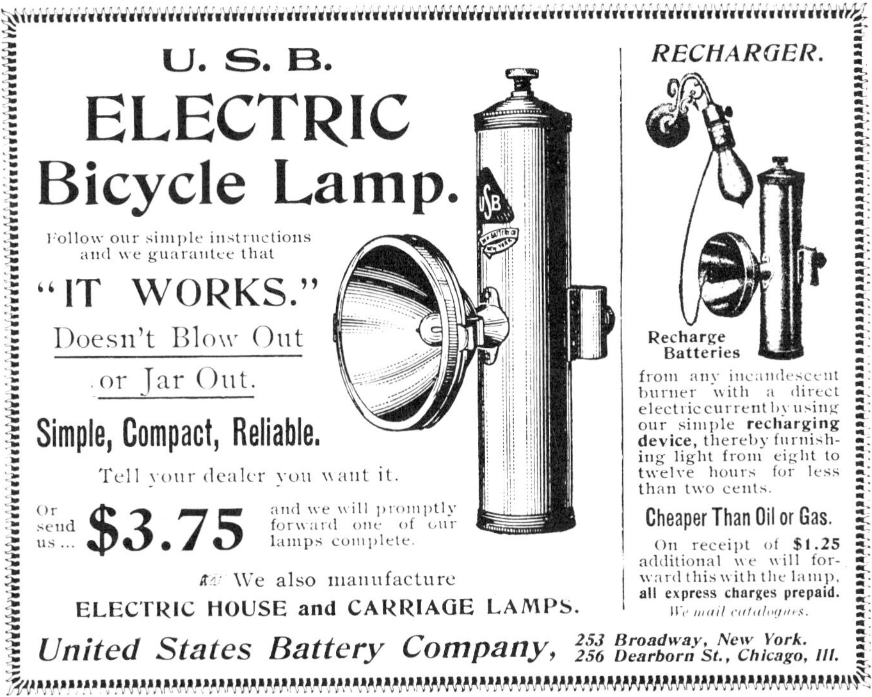

(1898)

Practicality was always good for a pitch in the days when do-it-yourselfing was fast becoming a bona fide American Tradition. Here's an "electric bicycle lamp" that rates one of the highest grass-roots accolades of all: "IT WORKS."

WANTED—BY A VERY HEALTHY, NEAT GIRL, a situation as wet nurse; her infant is ten days old; she has a fine breast of milk; can be highly recommended for sobriety, honesty, and moral conduct. Call at No. 120 Waverley-place.

The want ads of Way Back Then, like those of today, were among the few ads that were not illustrated (public announcements by government agencies and a very small percentage of "display ads" were and are also "word-only" sellers). Here we have the case of a "very healthy, neat" milk-laden girl whose overflow, it appears, is up for sale. (Only babes in arms need apply.)

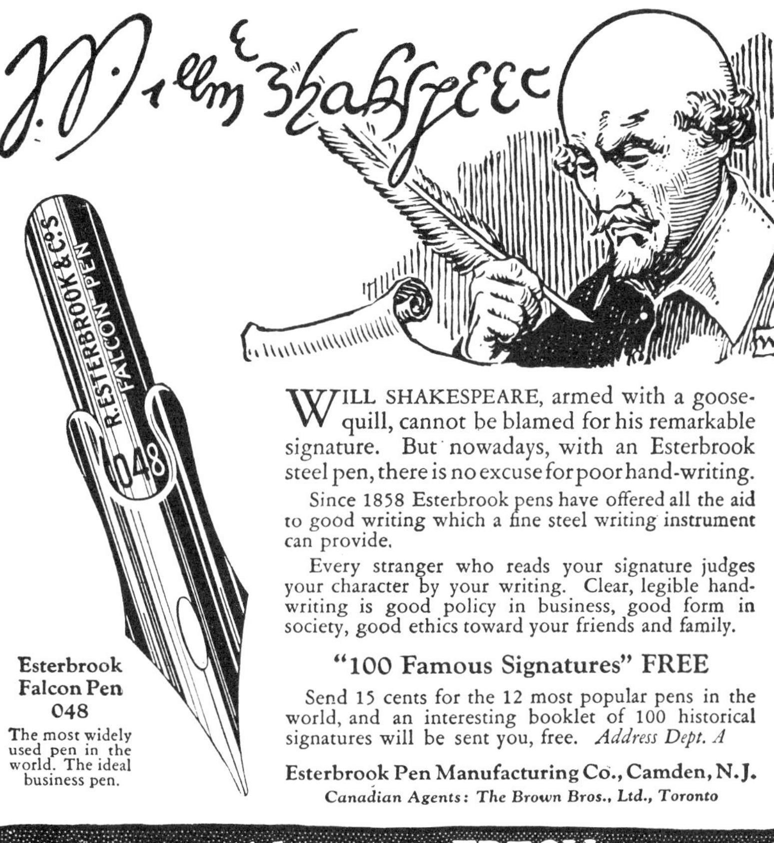

To the hucksters of yore, as to their modern counterparts, little was sacred. Even the ghost of the Bard himself somehow got conscripted into standing still for Esterbrook whilst they chidingly forgave him his scrawly hand.

As an illustration of the beneficial effects of AYER'S HAIR VIGOR, we refer to the case of Mrs. OLIVER DAVENPORT, of *Williamstown, Vt.*, aged 59 years, who at the age of twenty became bald, and remained so 38 years. During this time she tried many hair "restorers," with no effect. Coming by chance into possession of a part of a bottle of AYER'S HAIR VIGOR, she applied the liquid, and soon a downy growth of hair began to cover her head. With the use of less than four bottles more, she has now a fine growth of brown hair, twelve inches long, covering her head, except a small spot on top. This has starting upon it a downy growth, which Mrs. Davenport believes a persevering use of the VIGOR will cause to become abundant like the rest. This statement will be verified by the postmaster of Williamstown; also by the editor of the Northfield, Vt., *News.*

(1885)

A sample of Prof. Robb's Curlique will be sent free to any address. The Curlique will curl the straightest hair on the first application, (without injury) in soft, luxuriant, beautiful flowing curls. Address, with Stamp,

896-5t   Prof. B. H. ROBB, Parkman, Ohio.

(1870)

Here the pitch is hair. Does hair — or its lack — bug you no end? Then grow more of it. Or cover it up. Or curl it. Whatever: the mess is the message.

White
Ostrich Feathers

"White ostrich feathers are easily cleaned by soaking five minutes in warm suds made from Fairy Soap. Draw them lightly through the hand, rinse in warm, clear water, and dry by shaking over the stove. Re-curl by drawing each little barb over the dull edge of a knife or scissors."—*Mrs. Sarah Tyson Rorer.*

FAIRY SOAP

PURE—WHITE—FLOATING.

The Soap of the Century

Sold everywhere in three convenient sizes for the toilet, bath and laundry.

FREE Send us your name, address, and five Fairy Soap wrappers, to nearest office below, and we will mail you free a copy of a beautiful painting in water colors entitled "Fairy Tales," by the celebrated artist, Leon Moran. Size 17½x24 in. without lettering, ready for framing.

THE N. K. FAIRBANK COMPANY,
Chicago. St. Louis. New York. Boston. Philadelphia. Pittsburgh. Baltimore.

(1896)

Let's hear it for "FAIRY SOAP...The Soap of the Century." Just the thing for getting your white ostrich feathers looking good. What's more, a buyer of five bars could mail in the wrappers and get back free "a beautiful painting in water colors entitled 'Fairy Tales.'"

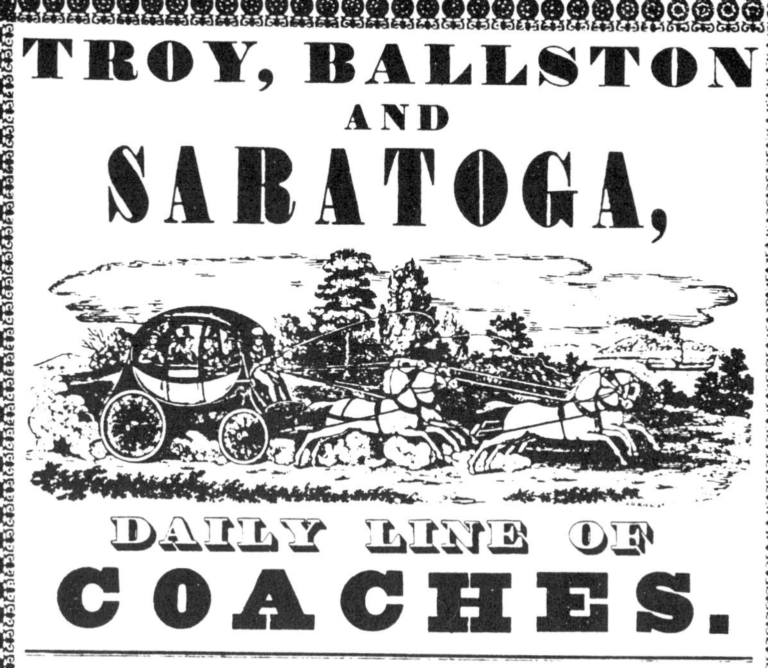

(1834)

Stagecoach announcements were a staple of newspaper and poster advertising all through the first half of the nineteenth century. The poster above, featuring the woodcut artistry of John H. Hall, is a superb example of how typefaces grew increasingly visual, as they were made to blend with, and counterpoint, the illustrations.

After the Honeymoon.

Their honeymoon was over,
The timothy and clover
    In all the summer fields was
    turning brown.
'Twas morning, she sat sighing ;
Bedewed with dismal crying
    She puckered up her fore-
    head in a frown.
Floors sadly needed scrubbing,
Black kettles needed rubbing,
    Her castles in the air had
    toppled down.
When lo ! a great magician transformed this sad condition,
    For **Gold Dust Washing Powder's** wide renown
Induced this bride to buy it—as soon as she could try it
    No happier home existed in the town.

Gold Dust Washing Powder

Sold everywhere.   Cleans everything.   Pleases everybody.

Here we see sown the seeds of the Soap Opera Syndrome, or How to Keep Wifie's Drudgery to a Magical Minimum. "After the Honeymoon" is the name of this parable in poesy. And as Samuel Goldwyn might once have said, "If the Muse were alive today, she'd be turning over in her grave!"

Appreciated.

ALAS poor Jumbo! But Messrs. Barnum, Bailey and Hutchinson, are still the owners of over fifty Elephants. In their travels we have reason to believe that all of these intelligent beasts carry **Centaur Liniment** in their trunks.

This is What Barnum Says.

438 Fifth Ave., New York, May 9, 1875.

"  **MONG** my vast troop of teamsters, equestrians, horses, camels and elephants, there are always some lame, wounded, galled and strained. My doctors and veterinaries all assure me that nothing has proven so prompt and efficacious a remedy for men and animals as **Centaur Liniment.** If you could supply me with a live Centaur, I will give you my check for $100,000."

P. T. BARNUM.

Jumbo and the Baby Elephant.

Centaur Liniment, anyone? It's just the thing for lame elephants and such — with no less than the great Barnum himself to vouch for its efficacy. And how fittingly Barnumesque is his tacked-on offer: "If you could supply me with a live Centaur, I will give you my check for $100,000." Beautiful!

What's My Line? would have had a field day with *these* two gents. I mean, just looking at them, would they strike *you* as being a pair of bonnet bleachers?

Old-time ad humor was almost always vivid and bold, even if, upon occasion, the message itself remained a *mite* obscure. Like what, you may ask, does "As Full as a Tick" suppose to mean in the above context? Don't ask.

Then again, there were moments when the pointed wryness of the rendering reached classic plateaus, as in this timeless, soft-soaped gem of political satire, turn-of-the-century style—a shot of shared insight paving (or laving) the way for The Sell.

There are Ivoryless men in this country!

There are men who still go along from day to day deep-sea-diving in the tub for a sunken, slippery parallelepiped. When they finally retrieve it and rub it heartily against their manly frames, it reluctantly deposits a thin, sticky coating that they, in all innocence, think is lather.

We want the attention of these men for ten seconds.

We want them to understand that real lather—Ivory lather—is a three-dimensioned product particularly distinguished by thickness. It develops as quickly as pride after a twelve-foot putt. It disappears in the rinse like a platform after election day.

And when the Ivory cake slips its moorings, it remains on the surface, to be recaptured on sight without a search warrant.

Give these matters a thought, gentlemen. They have much to do with the change from the Saturday night duty to the daily morning luxury.

PROCTER & GAMBLE

IVORY SOAP

99 ⁴⁴/₁₀₀ % PURE   IT FLOATS

ALL the fees from a Board of Directors meeting couldn't buy a finer cake of soap for face and hands than Guest Ivory, the new cake of Ivory made especially for the washstand. Just the right size for either the right or the left hand. Five cents.

This ad, from a 1924 issue of *The American Magazine,* is the least "old-time" of those collected here: it serves as a bridge between the primitive pioneers of before and today's more sophisticated breed. Full flowering of the "slick" school would soon come in the pages of such style-setting periodicals as *Vogue, Harper's Bazaar* and *The New Yorker.*

II Sample ads from two random years: 1896 and 1906

1896

ENTERPRISE

Raisin

and GRAPE

Seeder

Takes out every seed without destroying the shape of the Raisin. So simple that a child can do it.

Saves Time, Labor, Patience.

Avoids Appendicitis.

An ingenious machine — Always ready for use — Lasts a lifetime — Never gets out of order — Easily cleaned — Made in several sizes — No. 36, for ordinary family use, seeds a pound in five minutes.

Price $1.00 at Hardware Stores.

Send two 2-cent stamps for the "ENTERPRISING HOUSEKEEPER" — 200 recipes.

THE ENTERPRISE MFG. CO. OF PA.,

Philadelphia, Pa.

Makers of the Enterprise Meat Choppers.

"A sailor's wife, a sailor's joy should be,"
Yo-ho, Yo-ho!
But when he does the work at sea
His aid, like hers, is sure to be
Sap-o,li-o!

Business Suit, $10.

Warranted all Wool.

Choice of Light or Dark Mixed Cassimeres. Blue or Black Fine Twill Serges.

These Suits are Sewed with Silk, Buttonholes Silk-worked, Buttons sewed strongly with linen thread. No "Job Lots" of Woolens ever enter our factory. We do not buy the "mistakes" of the woolen mills.

Fashionable Cut.

Made for best trade. You run no risk in buying Cloth-. ing of us.

We have a reputation at stake. For 28 years we have been large makers and retailers of Clothing in New York and Brooklyn.

Illustrated Catalogue Free. Samples and measurement rules—to insure correct size—on request. Men's Suits, **$10 to $30.** Spring Overcoats, **$10 to $28.** Boys' Suits, **$2.75 up.** Boys' Sailor Suits, Shirt Waists, Hats, Caps, Collars, Cuffs, Shirts, Juvenile Suits, Bicycle Suits, Sweaters, Mackintoshes.

Baldwin the Clothier,

Manufacturers and Retailers,

Fulton and Smith Streets, Brooklyn, N. Y.

P. S.—No matter where you are you can deal safely with BALDWIN. Money with order is simplest. Refunded if goods do not please.

STEEL PICKET LAWN FENCE,

steel gates, steel posts and rail, also Field and Hog Fence Wire, single and double farm gates. For further information, write to the

UNION FENCE CO., De Kalb, Ill.

A sick woman cannot expect to have a healthy baby. An unhealthy baby has not the same chance for living as a healthy baby. The mother's condition must of necessity tell on the child's health and happiness. The laws of heredity are inflexible. The mother's weakness will surely show in some way in her child. A mother can make her child's life happy and successful, or miserable and a failure. She can do it by making and keeping herself perfectly strong and healthy during the period of gestation. She can do this by taking Doctor Pierce's Favorite Prescription. It is a most wonderful cure for all forms of female weakness and disease, and perhaps its greatest usefulness is in preparing for the trials and dangers of child-birth. It is a strengthening, purifying tonic. It acts directly on the organs distinctly feminine, drives out all impurities, promotes regularity and restores hearty, vigorous health. It will positively cure any form of female weakness or disease. It is the preparation of a regular, medical practitioner, whose great success as a specialist in the treatment of diseases of women has made him famous all over the world. Dr. Pierce is now, and has been for thirty years, chief consulting physician in the Invalids' Hotel and Surgical Institute, at Buffalo, N. Y.

Complete information about the "Favorite Prescription" is to be found in Dr. Pierce's "Common Sense Medical Adviser," several chapters of which are devoted to the reproductive physiology of women. A handsome volume of 1008 pages, and over 300 illustrations. It contains more exact information about the human body in health and disease than any other medical book. Hundreds of useful, simple receipts for the cure of many ailments that come to every family. Its statements are to be absolutely relied upon, and if followed will save many a doctor's bill. A new edition of half a million copies of this book is now being distributed free, bound in strong paper covers. Any one may have a copy who will send 21 cents in one-cent stamps, to pay cost of mailing *only*, to World's Dispensary Medical Association, Buffalo, N. Y. French cloth binding is 31 cents.

44

FLOWERS FOR WINTER BLOOMING.

What You Can Buy for 50 Cents, by Mail, Post Paid.
ALL THESE BULBS WILL BLOOM THIS WINTER.

Set A-10 Best Double Hyacinths, 10 kinds, . . . 50c
" B-10 Best Single Hyacinths, 10 kinds, ... 50c
" C- 5 Single and 5 Double Hyacinths, 10 kinds, 50c
" D-12 Ass't Hyacinths, D'ble, Single & Roman, 50c
" E-15 Choicest Varieties Narcissus, ... 50c
" F-35 Best Double Tulips, all different, . . . 50c
" G-35 Best Single Tulips, all different, . . . 50c
" H-40 Ass't Tulips, Double, Single and Parrot, 50c

Set J-60 Crocus, all colors, handsome, ... 50c
" K- 4 Chinese Sacred Lilies, ... 50c
" L-10 Choice Winter Blooming Roses, . . . 50c
" M-10 Choice Geraniums, all different, . . . 50c
" O- 6 Carnations, ready to bloom, ... 50c
" P-12 Choice Prize Winning Chrysanthemums, 50c
" S- 4 Elegant Decorative Palms, ... 50c

You may select half of any two sets for 50 cents, or 3 complete sets for $1.25; any 5 sets for $2.00; the entire 15 sets for $5.00; or half of each set for $2.50. Get your neighbor to club with you and get yours FREE. Our catalogue free. ORDER TO-DAY. **THE GREAT WESTERN PLANT CO., Springfield, Ohio.**

TULIPS.   HYACINTHS.
CHOICE WINTER FLOWERING BULBS.

Sent by Mail, postpaid, at the following special prices:

3 lovely HYACINTHS, different colors, fine, for 10 cents.
6 " TULIPS, lovely sorts, all different, " 10 "
5 " NARCISSUS, " " " " 10 "
10 SPANISH IRIS, nothing finer in flowers, - " 10 "
10 CROCUS, 5 sorts, named, - - - - " 10 "
10 FREESIAS, fine mixed sorts, - - - - " 10 "
10 OXALIS, all different colors, - - - " 10 "
Or the whole 54 Bulbs, post-paid, for 50 Cents.

MY CATALOGUE, ELEGANTLY ILLUSTRATED, of all kinds of Plants and Bulbs, for Fall Planting and Winter Blooming, is now ready, and will be mailed **FREE,** to all who apply. Choicest Hyacinths, Tulips, Narcissus, and other Bulbs at greatly reduced prices. Write for it at once. Address,

MISS ELLA V. BAINES,
The Woman Florist,   SPRINGFIELD, OHIO.

To quickly introduce *DR. HOBBS SPECIALTIES* throughout the U. S. and Canadas, we make this liberal offer. We will give a *Solid Gold Ring* or a set (6) elegant solid silverplated *Tea Spoons* to every girl or woman who will dispose of 15 vials of Dr. Hobbs wonderful Little Liver Pills among friends at 10 cents a vial. Send no money in advance, simply send your name and address. We mail you the pills postpaid. When sold, you send us the money and we mail you the ring or spoons. We take the pills back if you can't sell them. We run all the risk. Address, HOBBS REMEDY CO., Dept. 16, CHICAGO.

Every Lady

Interested in Fancy Work should write for catalogue and price-list of Stamped Linens, Wash Embroidery Silks, Commenced pieces of Embroidery with Silks to finish, and all latest designs in Art Novelties and Embroidery Materials. It will be sent free to any address.

Chas. F. Hurm, 644 Race St., Cincinnati, O.

All Skin Disorders

from simple Pimples to obstinate Eczema and Tetter can be quickly and permanently cured by the simple application of

HEISKELL'S OINTMENT.

It makes the skin soft, smooth and healthy, producing a clear and brilliant complexion.
50c. per box at Druggists or by mail.
JOHNSTON, HOLLOWAY & CO.,
531 Commerce St.,   Philadelphia.

74 Platt St., CLEVELAND, OHIO.

New Fancy Work Book

Entitled **"Florence Home Needlework"** for 1896. Just issued. It gives explicit instructions for embroidering tea cloths, center pieces and doylies in all the newest and prettiest patterns, including latest designs in the Rose, Jewel, Delft, Empire, Festoon, Fruit, Wild Flower and Leaf Embroideries. It contains full information as to the correct shades of silk to be used for each design, and how to work the piece. Also gives directions for knitting Infant's Shirt and Cap and crocheting a Baby's Bonnet. 96 pages. Over 60 illustrations. Sent for 6 cents in stamps. Be sure to state that you want "Florence Home Needlework" for 1896.

NONOTUCK SILK CO., 61 Bridge Street, Florence, Mass.

40c. PATTERNS FOR 10c.

Any FOUR patterns, and this paper one year, 60 cents, post-paid.

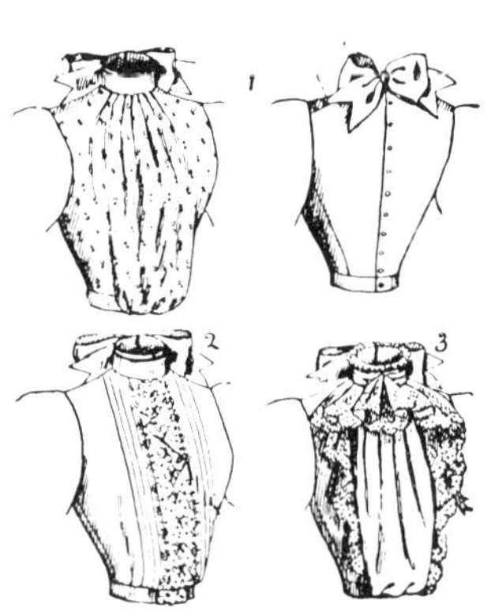

NO. 6822.—LADIES' AND MISSES' BLOUSE
VESTS.   10 cents.
Sizes, 32, 34, 36, 38 and 40 inches bust,
and 14 and 16 years.

NO. 6804.—CHILD'S FROCK. 10 cts.
Sizes, 4, 6, 8, 10 and 12 years.

NO. 6825.—LADIES' ETON JACKET. 10c.
Sizes, 32, 34, 36, 38, 40 and 42 inches bust.
NO. 6783.—LADIES' SKIRT. 11 cts.
Sizes, 22, 24, 26, 28 and 30 inches waist.

NO. 6776.—LADIES' TEA-GOWN. 11 cts.
Sizes, 32, 34, 36, 38, 40 and 42 inches bust.

Send for our large catalogue of cut paper patterns ; Free to any address.

LADIES HOME COMPANION, Springfield, Ohio.

HAIR ON THE FACE, NECK, ARMS OR ANY PART OF THE PERSON

QUICKLY DISSOLVED AND REMOVED WITH THE NEW SOLUTION

÷ MODENE ÷

AND THE GROWTH FOREVER DESTROYED WITHOUT THE SLIGHTEST INJURY OR DISCOLORATION OF THE MOST DELICATE SKIN.

Discovered by Accident.—IN COMPOUNDING, an incomplete mixture was accidentally spilled on the back of the hand, and on washing afterward it was discovered that the hair was completely removed. We purchased the new discovery and named it MODENE. It is perfectly pure, free from all injurious substances, and so simple any one can use it. It acts mildly but surely, and you will be surprised and delighted with the results. Apply for a few minutes and the hair disappears as if by magic. It has no resemblance whatever to any other preparation ever used for a like purpose, and no scientific discovery ever attained such wonderful results. **IT CAN NOT FAIL.** If the growth be light, one application will remove it permanently; the heavy growth such as the beard or hair on moles may require two or more applications before all the roots are destroyed, although all hair will be removed at each application, and without slightest injury or unpleasant feeling when applied or ever afterward. MODENE SUPERCEDES ELECTROLYSIS.

————*Recommended by all who have tested its merits—Used by people of refinement.*————

Gentlemen who do not appreciate nature's gift of a beard, will find a priceless boon in Modene, which does away with shaving. It dissolves and destroys the life principle of the hair, thereby rendering its future growth an utter impossibility, and is guaranteed to be as harmless as water to the skin. Young persons who find an embarrassing growth of hair coming, should use Modene to destroy its growth. Modene sent by mail, in safety mailing cases, postage paid, (securely sealed from observation) on receipt of price, **$1.00** per bottle. Send money by letter, with your full address written plainly. ☞ Correspondence sacredly private. Postage stamps received the same as cash. (ALWAYS MENTION YOUR COUNTY AND THIS PAPER.) Cut this advertisement out.

LOCAL AND GENERAL AGENTS WANTED. | **MODENE MANUFACTURING CO., CINCINNATI, O., U. S. A.** Manufacturers of the Highest Grade Hair Preparations. *You can register your letter at any Post-office to insure its safe delivery.*

We Offer $1,000 FOR FAILURE OR THE SLIGHTEST INJURY. ☞ EVERY BOTTLE GUARANTEED.

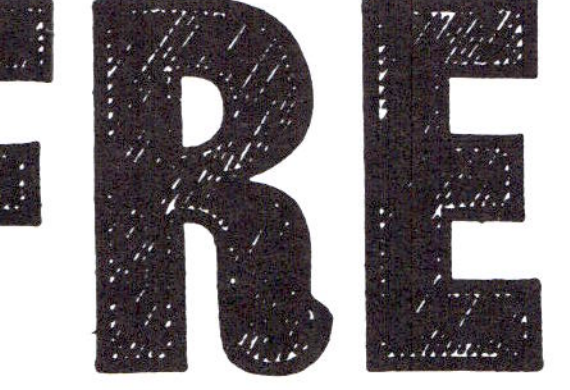

CATALOGUE
FREE
$160 00
Now is the time to buy a PIANO or ORGAN from the largest manufacturers in the world, who sell their instruments direct to the public at wholesale factory prices.
DON'T PAY a profit to agents and middlemen.
TERMS to suit all. No money asked in advance. Privilege of testing organ or piano in your own home 30 days. No expense to you if not satisfactory. Warranted 25 years.
REFERENCE Bank references furnished on application; the editor of this paper; any business man of this town, and to the thousands using our instruments in their homes. A book of testimonials sent with every catalogue. As an advertisement we will sell the first Piano in a place for only $160. Organs from $25 upwards.
Stool, Book, &c., FREE.
If you want to buy for cash,
If you want to buy on instalments,
BUT DON'T BUY UNTIL YOU
Write Us. BEETHOVEN PIANO & ORGAN CO.,
P. O. Box 657 WASHINGTON, N. J.

No Lame Back
No Aching Arms

.... IF YOU USE ....

WITCH KLOTH

THE MAGIC POLISHER.

The cost is next to nothing.
The work is next to nothing.
Nothing so dainty that **WITCH KLOTH** will injure it; no polished surface so dingy that **WITCH KLOTH** will not restore it.
The silverware, the bicycle, the piano, the glassware, the—anything you wish to polish comes bright as if by magic under its touch.

Sold by all { **Sample Kloth**, by mail, **15c.**
Retailers. { Witch Kloth Towels, 50c.

Asbury=Paine Mfg. Co., Wayne Junction, Phila.

If not for sale by local dealer, write
THE JOHN CHURCH CO., CINCINNATI or CHICAGO.

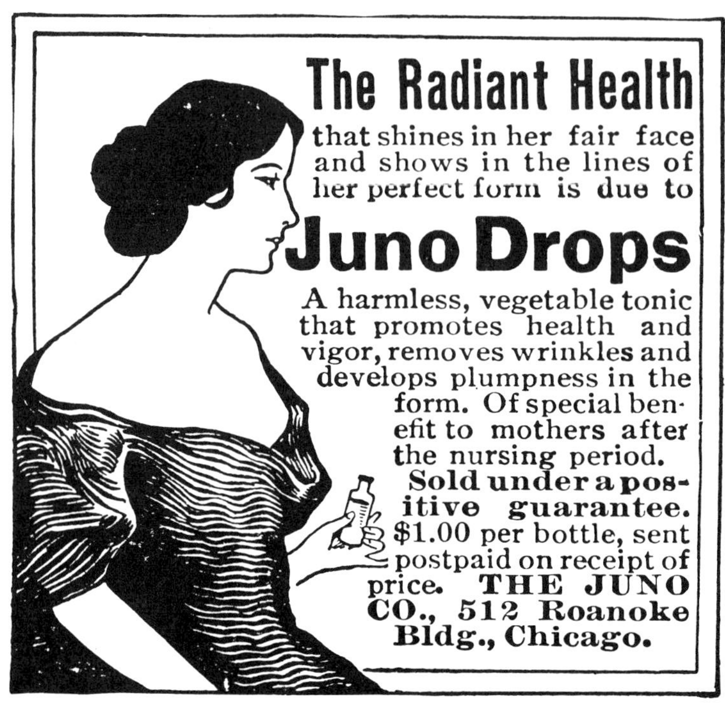

The Radiant Health
that shines in her fair face and shows in the lines of her perfect form is due to
Juno Drops
A harmless, vegetable tonic that promotes health and vigor, removes wrinkles and develops plumpness in the form. Of special benefit to mothers after the nursing period. Sold under a positive guarantee. $1.00 per bottle, sent postpaid on receipt of price. THE JUNO CO., 512 Roanoke Bldg., Chicago.

ME-GRIM-INE
A positive and permanent cure for
ME-GRIM (A Half-Headache)
and all other forms of
Headache or Neuralgia.
Headache Cured Free
by sample mailed you if this paper is mentioned. The more promptly headaches are relieved the less frequent will be their return until permanently cured. Sold by all druggists. 50 CENTS PER BOX.
The Dr. Whitehall Meg. Co.
South Bend, Ind.

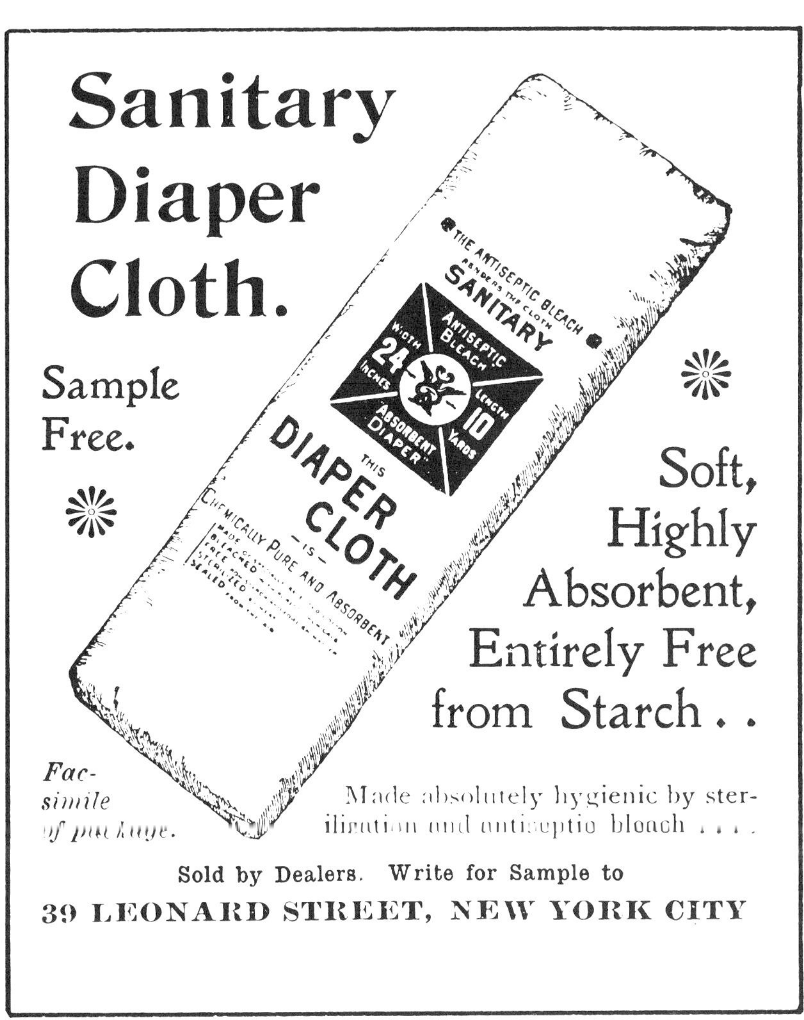

Sanitary
Diaper
Cloth.

Sample
Free.

Soft,
Highly
Absorbent,
Entirely Free
from Starch . .

THE ANTISEPTIC BLEACH RENDERS THE CLOTH
SANITARY
ANTISEPTIC BLEACH
WIDTH 24 INCHES
LENGTH 10 YARDS
ABSORBENT DIAPER
THIS DIAPER CLOTH IS
CHEMICALLY PURE AND ABSORBENT

Fac-
simile
of package.

Made absolutely hygienic by ster-
ilization and antiseptic bleach . . . .

Sold by Dealers. Write for Sample to
39 LEONARD STREET, NEW YORK CITY

SPECIAL SALE OF 10,000 LARGE POWERFUL ACHROMATIC TELESCOPES.

Positively such a good Telescope was never sold for this price before. THESE TELESCOPES ARE MADE BY ONE OF THE LARGEST MANUFACTURERS OF EUROPE, MEASURE CLOSED **12** INCHES AND OPEN OVER **3** FEET IN **4** SECTIONS. They are nicely **brass bound, brass safety cap** on each end to exclude dust, etc. with **powerful lenses,** scientifically ground and adjusted. **Guaranteed by the maker.** Heretofore, Telescopes of this size have been sold for from $5.00 to $8.00. Every sojourner in the country or at seaside resorts should certainly secure one of these instruments, and no farmer should be without one. Objec's miles away are brought to view with astonishing clearness. Sent by mail or express, safely packed, prepaid for only **99 cts.** Our new Catalogue of Watches, etc. sent with each order. This is a grand offer and you should not miss it. **We warrant** each Telescope **just as represented** or money refunded. **A customer writes:** from "Fulton, N.Y. March 27—Gents, received your Telescope; am very much pleased with it; it is all you recommend it to be.—J. L. HANARTS." Send **99 cents** by Registered Letter, Post Office Money Order, Express Money Order, or Bank Draft payable to our order. Address, **EXCELSIOR IMPORTING CO.,** Dept M K **Excelsior Building, New York City, Box 783.**

NO=TO=BAC GUARANTEED TOBACCO HABIT CURE

Over 1,000,000 boxes sold. 300,000 cures prove its power to destroy the desire for tobacco in any form. No-To-Bac is the greatest nerve-food in the world. Many gain 10 pounds in 10 days and it never fails to make the weak impotent man strong, vigorous and magnetic. Just try a box. You will be delighted. We expect you to believe what we say, for a cure is absolutely guaranteed by druggists everywhere. Send for our booklet, "Don't Tobacco Spit and Smoke Your Life Away," written guarantee and free sample. Address **THE STERLING REMEDY CO., Chicago or New York.**   123

SPECIAL FALL LINE FREE SAMPLES
Good Papers 3c

Beautiful Bed-room Papers 5 and 6 cts. Our high grade "Specials," 10c. and up. Largest **Wall Paper** stock in United States. **4,000,000 rolls.** New and exclusive designs. Samples, and booklet, "Points on Papering," mailed postpaid, only to those who describe rooms they wish to paper and colors desired. **Agents Wanted.** We want to establish an agency, with exclusive privileges, in every town, to sell from large sample books. Agents' complete outfit, $1.00.

UNITED STATES WALL PAPER CO., 421 Race Street, Cincinnati, Ohio.

With Root's Home Rep'ng Outfits for half-soling and rep'ng Boots, Shoes, Rubbers, Harness, Tinware, etc. No. 1, 40 items, $3; No. 2, 32 items, $2. Send for FREE catalog describing these and "Root's Simplicity Process" for home rep'ng. Carpenters' and Blacksmiths' tools, etc. Agents wanted. THE ROOT BROS. CO. Box F, Plymouth, O

WORLD POCKET STOVE

Will Keep Your Hands Warm.

3½ in. in diameter, nickel-plated. A perfect portable heater. Fits any pocket and will burn anywhere. For Skaters, Coasters, Drivers, Postmen, Policemen, Ladies, when calling or driving, School Children, etc. Lasts a lifetime, perfectly safe and requires but a few seconds to light. One carbon will burn two hours and gives no flame, smoke or unpleasant odor. Complete, with 12 carbons, $1.00, post-paid.

PECK & SNYDER, 130 Nassau Street, NEW YORK.

1906

An Achievement in Writing Paper Making Which All Women of Taste Will Appreciate

Eaton's Hot-Pressed Vellum

For the first time in the history of paper making, we are able to announce a hot-pressed writing paper at a price which makes it available for correspondence use.

Heretofore hot-pressed paper has been used exclusively as a drawing paper by artists. The expense incident to producing it —a long, tedious method by which the finest quality of paper was pressed, sheet by sheet, between hot plates—has precluded its use for correspondence.

Our process is an adaptation of this famous old, hot-pressed method. It produces the same results and yet puts the price within reach of all. In Eaton's Hot-Pressed Vellum, you get not only a perfect writing surface, but also an effect that is at once refined, dainty and distinctive.

Good form in letter writing demands the use of the most fashionable papers. Eaton's Hot-Pressed Vellum and its rougher companion—Eaton's Cold-Pressed Linen—are the newest as well as the most correct styles in writing papers.

Every woman who wishes to see this newest style in writing paper and cannot yet secure it easily from her own stationer, may send 25 cents to us and receive a sample one-half quire of either the Linen or the Vellum, assorted in two sizes of paper and envelopes.

Eaton-Hurlbut Paper Company,

Dept. 12.   Pittsfield, Mass.

Ask dealer for it.

Makes blacking a stove a pleasure. Easily applied, safe—clean—economical—goes twice as far as other polishes.

FREE SAMPLE *Address Dept. C.*

Lamont, Corliss & Co., Agts., 78 Hudson St., New York

40 Complete Novels, Novelettes and Stories for Only 6 Cents

For the purpose of introducing our popular publications and securing new customers for them, we will send by mail post-paid to any address, upon receipt of only **Six Cents** in postage stamps, **Forty Complete Novels, Novelettes and Stories** by Popular Authors, as follows: *A Terrible Repentance*, by Charlotte M. Braeme; *Woven on Fate's Loom*, by Charles Garvice; *In Daffodil Time*, by Effie Adelaide Rowlands; *The Tide on the Moaning Bar*, by Frances Hodgson Burnett; *The House in the Wood*, by Mrs. Jane G. Austin; *Maggie Lee*, by Mrs. Mary J. Holmes; *The Sapphire Circlet*, by Anna Katharine Green; *A True Story*, by Mark Twain; *The Parson at Jackman's Gulch*, by A. Conan Doyle; *Headleigh Hall*, by Mrs. Emma D. E. N. Southworth; *Huldah*, by Marion Harland; *The Last of the Mountjoys*, by Mrs. May Agnes Fleming; *Samantha in Washington*, by Josiah Allen's Wife; *Elsie Latimer's Sacrifice*, by Amanda M. Douglas; *The St. Hildric Diamonds*, by Emma Garrison Jones; *Sold for Naught*, by Mrs. Amelia E. Barr; *The Mystery at Calthorpe Hall*, by Charlotte M. Braeme; *The Twelve Wine Glasses*, by Mrs. Mary J. Holmes; *My Host at C.*, by Anna Katharine Green; *A Literary Nightmare*, by Mark Twain; *Alabama Joe*, by A. Conan Doyle; *Under the Laurels*, by Mrs Alex. McVeigh Miller; *Monica*, by "The Duchess"; *The Mummy's Curse*, by Louisa M. Alcott; *The Bar Lighthouse*, by Mary E. Wilkins; *Throgmorton Haggett's Discovery*, by Julian Hawthorne; *Codago*, by John Habberton; *Plotting for a Husband*, by Helen Corwin Pierce; *The Turning of the Worm*, by Ella Higginson; *The Criminal Witness*, by Sylvanus Cobb, Jr.; *A Terrible Retribution*, by Emerson Bennett; *The Drunkard's Wife*, by Mary Kyle Dallas; *The Heart of a Maid*, by Etta W. Pierce; *The Detective's Ghost*, by Clarence M. Boutelle; *John Beckwith's Reverses*, by Horatio Alger, Jr.; *Lost in the Woods*, by Edward S. Ellis; *Across the Plains*, by Virginia F. Townsend; *Dorothy's Dilemma*, by Hayden Carruth; *The Lottery Ticket*, by Mrs. Jennie Davis Burton, and *The Fatal Ride*, by Esther Serle Kenneth. Bear in mind that we send the entire collection of *Forty Complete Novels, Novelettes and Stories* by mail post-paid upon receipt of *Six Cents*. This is purely an introductory offer; we make no profit. Satisfaction is guaranteed or money will be refunded. Address: **F. M. LUPTON, Publisher, No. 27 City Hall Place, New York.**

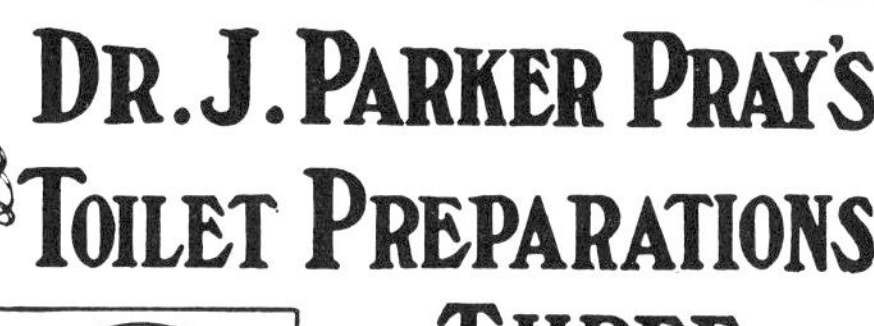

Dr. J. Parker Pray's
Toilet Preparations
Three Graces

Established 1868

CREAM VAN OLA

For softening and whitening the skin. Feeds and nourishes the tissues, and is considered the standard by the fastidious. Jars, 25 cents.

ROSALINE

Cannot be detected, gives the face and nails a delicate rose tint that is truly beautiful. ROSALINE is not affected by perspiration or displaced by bathing. Jars, 25 cents.

ONGOLINE

Bleaches and cleans the nails, removes ink, hosiery and glove stains from the skin; guaranteed harmless. Bottles, 50 cents.

Send stamp for illustrated catalogue of prices.

Goods sent on receipt of price and postage.

Dr. J. Parker Pray Co.

Sole Manufacturers and Proprietors,

10 and 12 East 23d Street, NEW YORK CITY·

PARKER'S Arctic Socks
(TRADE MARK) Reg.

Healthful for bed-chamber, bath and sick-room. Worn in rubber boots, absorbs perspiration. Made of knitted fabric, lined with soft white wool fleece. Sold in all sizes by dealers or by mail, 25c a pair. Parker pays postage.

Catalogue free. **Look for Parker's name in every pair.**
J. H. Parker, Dept. 27, 25 James St., Malden, Mass.

AUTHORS, ATTENTION! Write a Song

Fortunes are made annually. We write Music to your words. Arrange, secure publication, Copyright, etc.

Vincennes Music Co., Dept. K, 5647 Prairie Ave., Chicago, Ill.

WHEN YOU BUY
A Rain Coat

Rainy Day Suit, Skirt, or the cloth from which to make any of these garments, insist on having the genuine

"*Cravenette*"

You'll know it by this circular ☞ trade-mark stamped on the back of the cloth,

or *Cravenette* label on garment.

Write for booklet H. H.

B. Priestley & Co.

71 Grand Street, NEW YORK.

HOW TO GET TWO EMBROIDERED SHIRT WAIST PATTERNS FREE!

ANOTHER SPECIAL OFFER! In forwarding your subscription to THE LADIES' WORLD, if you will send us the names and addresses of five ladies who are interested in women's publications, but who, as far as you know, are not acquainted with our magazine, we

Eyelet Design. Price 35 Cents

Floral Design. Price 35 Cents

will send you **free and postpaid,** to pay you for your trouble, the two handsome Embroidered Shirt Waist Patterns, as shown in the illustrations, which are worth at retail 70 cents. The designs are the very latest, are perforated on parchment paper, and can be used over and over again. We also include the necessary material for making the transfers. Address all orders:

S. H. MOORE COMPANY, (Dept. A) 23 to 27 City Hall Place, New York

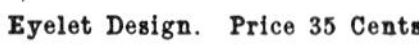

100 Visiting Cards Post Paid 50c

Also Business, Mourning, Birth, Fraternal, Professional and Emblematic. We have cuts of trade marks and emblems for all railroads, lodges and fraternal societies. Monogram Stationery. Wedding Invitations and Announcements. Samples free.
E. J. Schuster Ptg. & Eng. Co., Dept. AF, St. Louis, Mo.

Your Gas Bills Cut in Two

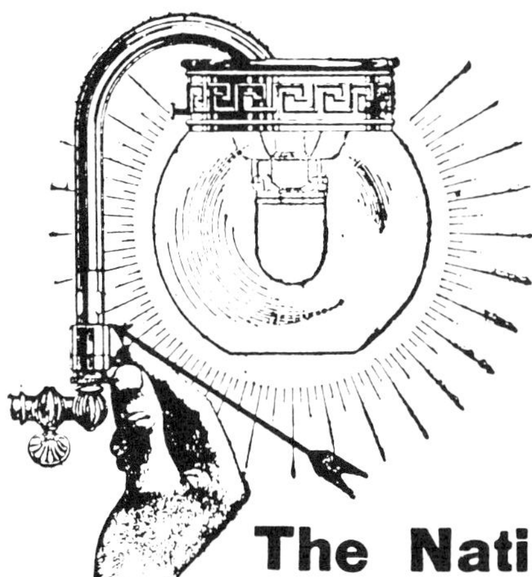

You Are Using More Gas Than You Need!

You Are Breaking Too Many Globes!

You Are Wasting Too Many Mantles!

because the pressure forces more gas through the pipes than is necessary to give you a good, steady, bright light.

The National Automatic Gas Light (Inverted)

has an automatic regulator which allows just enough gas (not too much or too little) to pass through at all times to make a perfect light, which prevents the wasting of gas, breaking of globes and mantles, and destruction of burners.

The National Automatic Gas Light gives a steady, full light downward of twice the candle power at half the cost of the vertical light and one-fifth the cost of electricity.

The National is the only light that is sold under a positive guarantee to do what we claim or money refunded.

Try One on Two Weeks' Free Trial

Under our guarantee you take no risk. Any dealer in lighting devices can supply you with the National at $1.75 each, boxed complete, or send direct for handsome booklet—"Seven Stages in Lighting."

THE NATIONAL GAS LIGHT CO.
1209 Porter St., Kalamazoo, Michigan

Caution: Insist on getting the National. Accept no other. The words—National Automatic—stamped on every regulator. You can see the pin point jump when the gas is turned on. Look for these features before purchasing.

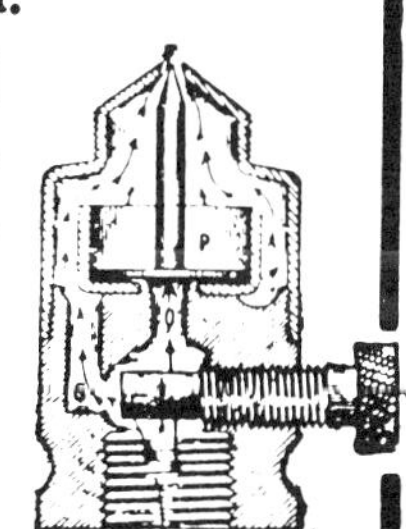

Automatic Regulator

The device that makes the inverted gas light a success.

Dainty Desserts

For quickly made luncheon or any hasty collation by the use of a

JUNKET

Tablet added to a small quantity of milk. One tablet makes a quart of savory custard or ice cream. By varying the flavors, a great variety of delicious desserts can be made. Ten tablets with full directions for use 10 cents. Sold by Grocers. Booklet free.

Chr. Hansen's Laboratory, P. O. Box 2550, Little Falls, N. Y.

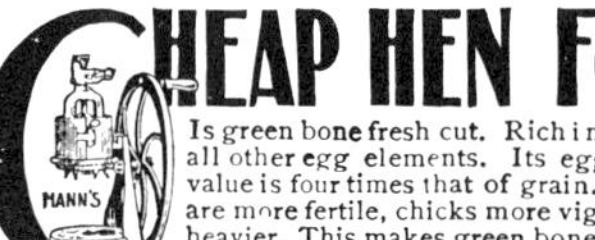

Is green bone fresh cut. Rich in protein and all other egg elements. Its egg producing value is four times that of grain. The eggs are more fertile, chicks more vigorous, fowls heavier. This makes green bone cheap food.

Mann's Latest Model Bone Cutter.

Cuts all bone, meat and gristle. Never clogs. **10 DAYS FREE TRIAL.** No money in advance. Cat'lg free.

F. W. MANN CO., Box 46, MILFORD, MASS.

Anti-Crooked Heel Cushions

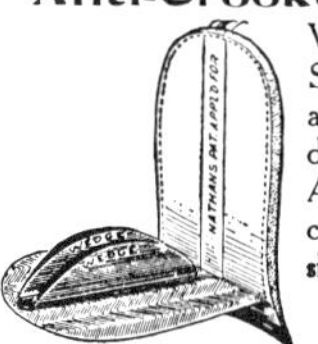

Will prevent running over the Heels of Shoes. Acts as a cushion and can be adjusted to make the wearer taller if so desired. Makes walking a pleasure. At all shoe stores or by mail on receipt of price, 50 cents per pair, any size, worn inside of shoes. Free circular.

NATHAN ANKLE SUPPORT CO.
88c Reade Street, New York.

VELVO CREAM takes out wrinkles and keeps them out. Makes the skin as smooth and soft as Velvet. If troubled send us 30 cents in stamps and get a large tube. It is a perfect Flesh Food. **Velvo Cream Co., Rochester, N. Y.**

This Bottle of
ED. PINAUD'S
Lilas de France
EXTRAIT VEGETAL
is yours

Send 10 cents (to pay postage and packing) and we will forward it to your address together with ED. PINAUD'S booklet, '' Messages from the Stars.'' Please mention your dealer's name when writing.

Ed. Pinaud's Lilas de France

is an exquisite and delightful perfume for the handkerchief, atomizer, bath and general toilet uses.

It is the most popular toilet preparation among women of fashion in Paris and New York—a single drop contains the fragrance of a bunch of freshly cut lilacs.

Indispensable to men after shaving

Parfumerie Ed. Pinaud

American Headquarters of Ed. Pinaud, Paris

Ed. Pinaud Building
85 Fifth Avenue, New York

HOSIERY FOR YOUR ENTIRE FAMILY
For $1.00

To introduce our 25c trade mark Hosiery

"Chilhowee" Brand

We will, upon receipt of $1.00, send postpaid, to any address in the U. S., seven pairs of high-class socks or stockings. You may take seven pairs of either men's, women's or children's, or assort your order to suit the needs of your family. In ordering state number of pairs of each size.

"Chilhowee" Twenty-five Cent Hosiery

is guaranteed fast black, seamless, reinforced heels and toes. Knit to fit from select quality yarns. With our cotton grown and spun, our Coal mined and Labor raised right here in Tennessee we produce the biggest value hosiery in the world, and want you to try it. Satisfaction or money refunded. Sample pair either kind sent on receipt of 25 cents.

CONSUMERS MDSE. CO.
115 Union Street,   **Knoxville, Tenn.**

SONG WRITERS

Your Poems May Be Worth **THOUSANDS OF DOLLARS** Send them to us today. We Will Compose the Music. Hayes Music Co., 80 Star Bldg., Chicago

The Question of Beauty

is largely a matter of skin cleanliness and healthfulness. Taboo paint, powder, skin foods, lotions and such—make friends with good soap and fresh water — take plenty of exercise— and Dame Nature will do her best for y o u r complexion.

Did you ever stop to think what happens when the skin is not kept thoroughly cleansed? (and when we say *cleansed*, we mean *cleansed*, not merely *washed off*.)

The surface of the human body contains millions of tiny little glands — only visible through a microscope — which are full of life and duty when in a healthful condition. One-sixth of all the waste matter daily thrown off from the body is shed through these pores, and if not thoroughly removed it remains to clog up these glands and destroy their mission. A sallow, "broken out" or generally unhealthy skin is the result.

Absolute skin health and beauty—and this means the daily removal of all waste matter—is only possible with the constant aid of good soap and water. The water is easily obtained ; the problem is to find the right soap.

A soap can either cleanse, purify, soften and beautify the skin—or it can clog, irritate, roughen and injure it.

FAIRY SOAP not only *cleans* but *cleanses*. It removes the dead waste matter—the impurities—from the pores and leaves them free to perform their function.

FAIRY SOAP is pure —it is made from choice cocoanut oil and *edible beef fat*—the best and purest ingredients we can buy. It contains no coloring matter or other adulterant to cover up a multitude of bad materials. It is good, pure soap and nothing but· soap, and will agree with the tenderest skin.

Although F A I R Y SOAP sells for but 5c a cake, it is the peer of any soap—white or otherwise —sold today, regardless of price. Prove this to your satisfaction by a personal test.

"Have You a Little Fairy in Your Home?"

POPULAR UNDERWEAR

Vellastic Utica Ribbed Fleece Underwear in Big Demand.

In the two years that Vellastic Underwear has been on the market, there has been such a steady increase in the popular call for this superior undergarment that the mills find it hard work to keep up with the demand.

Vellastic Underwear fills a long-felt want for a low-priced undergarment that will combine the conditions of ideal underwear. Vellastic Utica Ribbed Fleece Underwear is woven by a new method so that it is outwardly a ribbed and elastic fabric with a soft, downy fleece next the skin.

The beauty of Vellastic Underwear lies in the fact that it affords a snug, comfortable fit, while the fleece keeps the body warm and comfortable.

Prices: Men's and women's garments, 50c. Ladies' Union Suits, $1.00 each. Children's sizes in union suits at 50c or in two piece suits at 25c a garment.

The trade mark, Vellastic Utica Ribbed Fleece, is sewed on every garment. If not at your dealer's write us, giving us his name. Booklet and sample of fabric free.

Utica Knitting Company, Utica, N. Y.

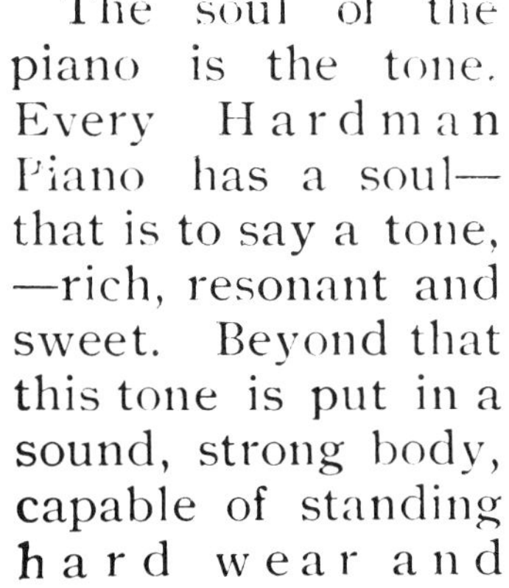

HARDMAN PIANO

The soul of the piano is the tone. Every Hardman Piano has a soul— that is to say a tone, —rich, resonant and sweet. Beyond that this tone is put in a sound, strong body, capable of standing hard wear and changes of climate.

Because of its soul—and the stanchness of its body, the Hardman is the piano par excellence for the home.

The
Hardman Autotone Piano

-the famous Hardman Upright Piano with the Hardman Piano-Player built within its case,- we claim is the best instrument of its kind made. Novice and musician can play it with equal skill. Let us tell you more about it.

Where we have no dealer we will send price lists and explain our easy payment system. We take old pianos in exchange.

Write us for our new booklet "Piano Helps" (postpaid).

Hardman, Peck & Co.

Established 1842.
Fifth Avenue and Nineteenth Street, New York.

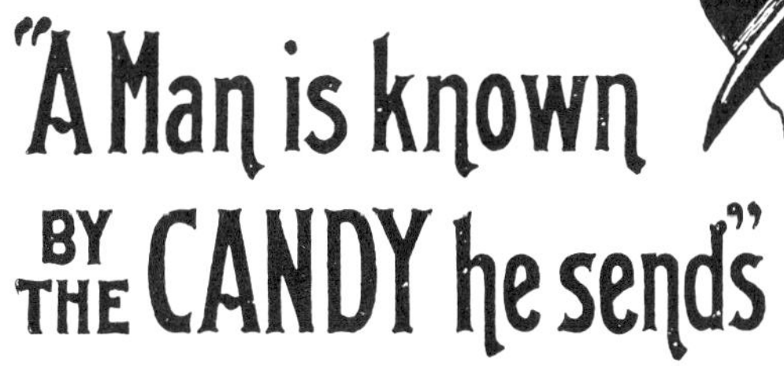

"A Man is known
BY THE CANDY he sends"

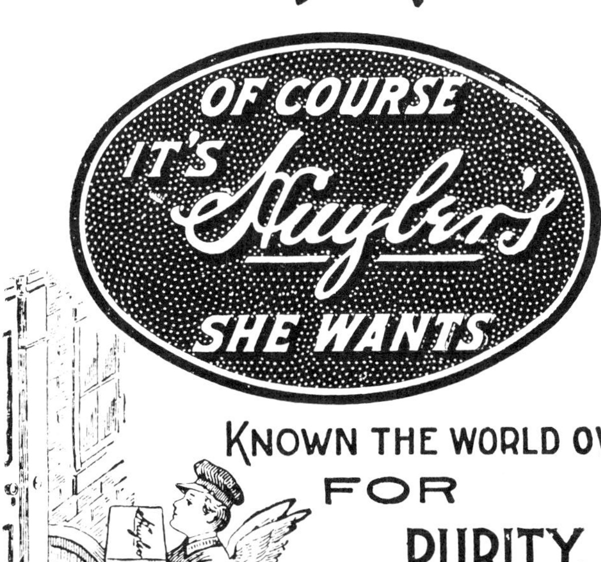

OF COURSE IT'S Huyler's SHE WANTS
KNOWN THE WORLD OVER
FOR
PURITY,
QUALITY & FLAVOR
Sold at our Stores & by
Sales Agents Everywhere.
THERE CAN BE NO MORE WELCOME
GIFT FOR OLD and YOUNG.

Stewart Hartshorn
HARTSHORN
SHADE ROLLERS
Bear the script name of Stewart
Hartshorn on label.
Wood Rollers.   Tin Rollers.

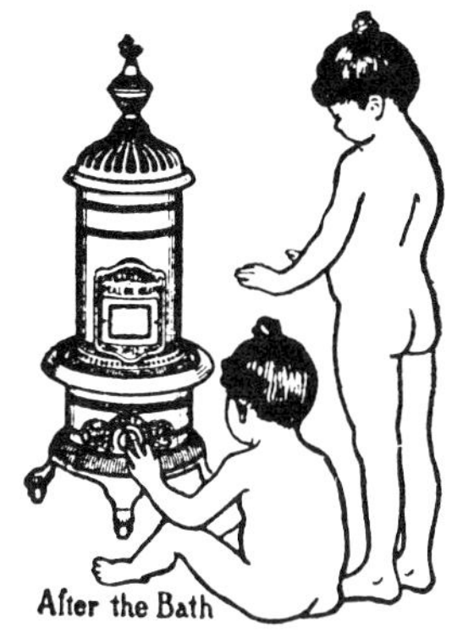

Buy a Barler

for quick clean heat that you can move anywhere and always have a warm room.

If you do not find it smokeless, odorless, saves work, heats fast= er and is better than any Oil Heater you have ever seen, re= turn it and it will not cost you a cent.

Write for Booklet and Trial Offer.

A. C. BARLER MFG. CO., 102 Lake St., Chicago.

Sent on Approval.   Send No Money.   **$1.50**
We Will Trust You 10 Days   Hair Switch

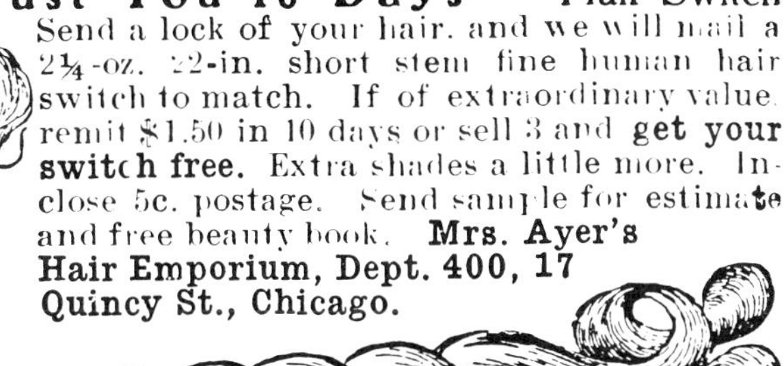

Send a lock of your hair. and we will mail a 2¼-oz. 22-in. short stem fine human hair switch to match. If of extraordinary value. remit $1.50 in 10 days or sell 3 and **get your switch free.** Extra shades a little more. In- close 5c. postage. Send sample for estimate and free beauty book. **Mrs. Ayer's Hair Emporium, Dept. 400, 17 Quincy St., Chicago.**

BE A SOCIETY EDITOR!

Do club. art, musical and other woman's work on a newspaper. Splendid field for young women. Our school. founded BY A WOMAN FOR WOMEN. gives practical newspaper training *by mail* Special rates to re- cent school and college graduates. Write now for particulars.

**Woman's Newspaper Training School, To'edo, Ohio
705 National Union Building, Huron St.**

WRITE THE *Words* FOR A *Song*

And we will write the music and present to BIG N.Y. Publishers
A HIT will make you RICH.   Send now for Free Booklet.
Metropolitan Music Co., 745 St. James Bldg., New York

Why Beans are so Rich in Nitrogen

PULL up a bean stalk and see.

Observe the little nodules clinging to its roots.

These have the unique power to seize free Nitrogen from the air and convert it into nitrates for the roots.

This Nitrogen in turn ascends, through the stalks, to the pods, and accumulates, as Nitrogenous Proteid, in the Beans.

That's *why* Beans are among the greatest of all Body-Builders.

Beans contain about *23 pounds* of Nitrogenous tissue and Muscle-making Proteid in every 100 pounds.

Bread contains only 6½ pounds, Bacon 8 pounds, Cream Cheese 8½ pounds, Eggs 12½ pounds, Beefsteak *20 pounds* per 100.

So that Beans are a much more powerful food for body-building and repair than even Beef, Eggs, Bacon, or other foods of many times their price.

Beans also contain three times as much Phosphorus as Beef, 2½ times as much as Eggs, and 4 times as much as Milk.

Phosphorus, you know, is the food-factor which feeds Nerves and Brain, and which is used up in *thinking.*

Beans also contain more of the Potash and Lime, from which Bone and Teeth are formed, than any other *vegetable* food.

Moreover, Beans, while being such magnificent tissue, muscle and bone builders, contain practically *no Fat.*

(There is a broad hint in this for Americans with a tendency to stoutness).

But, Beans, as usually served, have their fault.

That fault is a heavy surplus of useless *Sulphur.*

This Sulphur turns into Sulphuretted Hydrogen Gas when Beans are eaten.

And that Gas is what causes Flatulence, Colic, " wind on the Stomach."

And that is where the " Snider-Process" steps in—to eliminate such bean-faults.

That Process not only extracts the bitter principle (Natural to all Beans) but makes them mellow, cheesy and firm to the tooth, while *porous* as little sponges, so the Stomach Fluids can readily penetrate and *digest* them.

The "Snider-Process," in this way, *doubles* the *digestibility* of Beans without making them mushy, soft, split, squashed or discolored, like other brands of Pork and Beans.

The *porous* nature of "Snider-Process" Beans also permits them to evenly absorb the delicious Catsup in which they are immersed, with its dainty flavor of Seven Spices.

Buy a tin of "Snider-Process" Pork and Beans to-day.

Cut it open *before heating* and compare its perfect whole-bean contents with the *best* brand of Pork and Beans you have ever before used.

If it is not *better* than that *best*, take this advertisement to your Grocer as authority to get your money back.

That's an offer worth while, isn't it?

THE T. A. SNIDER PRESERVE CO., CINCINNATI, O.

The Motoriste is a most enthusiastic friend of lovely

Lansdowne

For it is the Dress Fabric which is not only delightful to wear but dust does not harm it and a night's hanging removes all the wrinkles.

Genuine perforated every 3 yards on the selvedge.

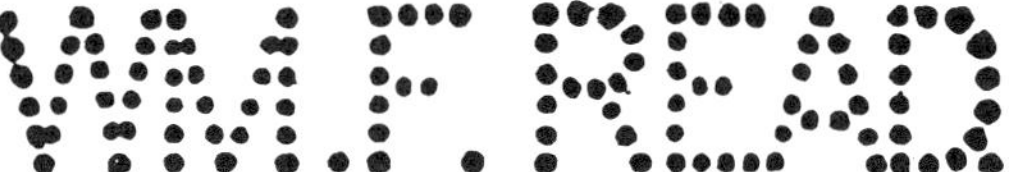

All Colors and Shades

For Sale at all Good Stores

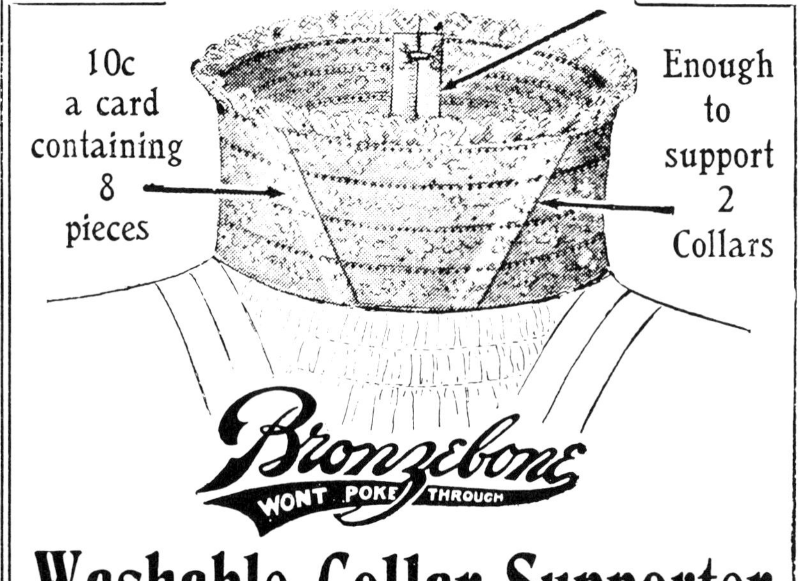

Washable Collar Supporter

Holds collar in shape and doesn't poke through or scratch the neck. Silk covered, with finished ends. Bends with every movement of the neck and is entirely comfortable. Washing won't twist, break or rust it.

More than 3.000.000 sets of **Bronzebone** sold in 2 years. At all better class stores. If your dealer hasn't it, send us his name and address with 10c and we'll mail you enough to support 2 collars. Specify color—white or black, and size—low, medium or high.

L. Hollander, Mfr., 724 Market Street, PHILADELPHIA.

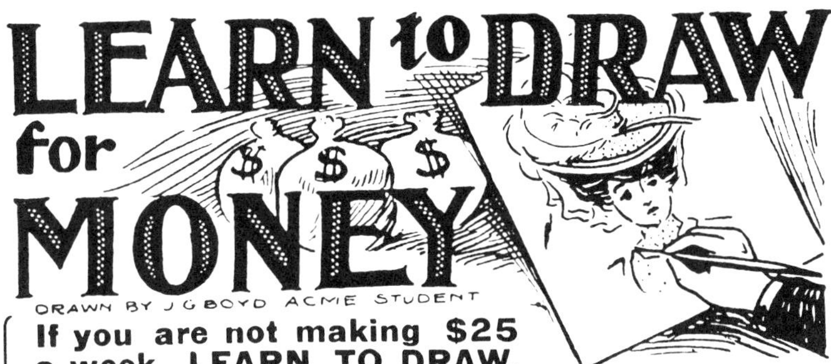

If you are not making $25 a week, LEARN TO DRAW.

Artists get high salaries. A man who can simply make good letters for commercial headings and advertisements can hold a good position. If you want to be

**A Commercial Designer and Letterer
A Cartoonist and Comic Artist
A Newspaper and Magazine Illustrator
A Mechanical Draftsman
An Architectural Draftsman
A Sheet Metal Pattern Draftsman
or a School Teacher of Drawing**

Let us train you at your home or in our resident School. Write now for full information. State course you wish to study. Correspondence or Resident Instruction. **THE ACME, SCHOOL OF DRAWING, 203 Chase Bl'k., Kalamazoo, Mich.**

IT PAYS men with small capital to give Public Exhibitions with a **MAGIC LANTERN, STEREOPTICON** or **MOVING PICTURE OUT-FIT.** Catalogue **free.**

McALLISTER, Mfg. Optician, 49 Nassau St., N. Y.

RELY ON THIS EYE

Don't be plagued with a constant fear that your waist gaps behind—fasten it with an eye to be relied upon.

PEET'S PATENT INVISIBLE EYES

are sure as fate—never let go, yet never show. Don't wear off, or tear off. Far better than any other eye, or than a silk loop.

It's all in the Triangle

Sold at all stores, all sizes, black or white. Always sold in envelopes, 5c. With spring hooks, 10c.

PEET BROS., Dept. F, Philadelphia, Pa.

Death's
Laboratory

Drawn by
E. W. Kemble

COLLIER'S EXPOSÉ
OF THE
PATENT MEDICINE FRAUD

Death's Laboratory
(A CARTOON)

June 3d "Patent medicines are poisoning people throughout America to-day. Babies who cry are fed laudanum under the name of syrup. Women are led to injure themselves for life by reading in the papers about the meaning of backache. Young men and boys are robbed and contaminated by vicious criminals who lure them to their dens through seductive advertisements."

Criminal Alliance of the Newspapers with Fraud and Poison

July 8th "Newspapers have done so much to create the success of 'fakes' in medicine that their duty is clearly to help remove them. It sounds high-minded for Journalism to bark ferociously against the reign of graft in politics or in high finance, but it can practice a little *real* reform, if it chooses, by canceling some of the most profitable results of its own limberness of conscience."

The Great American Fraud

October 7th "Gullible America will spend this year some seventy-five millions of dollars in the purchase of patent medicines. It will swallow huge quantities of alcohol, an appalling amount of opiates and narcotics, a wide assortment of varied drugs, ranging from powerful and dangerous heart depressants to insidious liver stimulants; and, far in excess of all other ingredients, undiluted fraud."

Peruna and the Bracers

October 28th "So well recognized is the use of Peruna for its alcoholic effects that a number of Southern papers advertise a cure for the 'Peruna habit.' What makes Peruna profitable to the maker and a curse to the community at large, is the fact that the minimum dose first ceases to satisfy; then the moderate dose, and finally the maximum dose; and the unsuspecting patron, who began with it as a medicine, goes on to use it as a beverage, and finally to be enslaved by it as a habit."

Conspiracy Against the Freedom of the Press

Nov. 4th "So it was no mean intellect which devised the scheme whereby every newspaper in America is made an active lobbyist for the Patent Medicine Association. The man who did it is the present president of the organization; its executive head in the work of suppressing public knowledge, stifling public opinion, and warding off public legislation."

Liquozone

Nov. 18th "Liquozone is sulphurous and sulphuric acids (corrosive poisons) heavily diluted; that is all. Will the compound destroy germs in the body? A series of tests conducted by the Lederle Laboratories answers the question in this summary: 'To summarize, we would say that *Liquozone had no curative effect*, but did, when given in pure form, lower the resistance of the animals so that they *died a little earlier than those not treated.*'"

The Subtle Poisons

Dec. 2d "Nostrums there are, which reach the thinking classes as well as the readily gulled. Depending as they do for their success upon the lure of some subtle drug concealed under a trade-mark name, or some opiate not readily obtainable under its own label, these are the most dangerous of all quack medicines, not only in their immediate effect. but because they create enslaving appetites, sometimes obscure and difficult of treatment; most often, tragically obvious. Of these concealed drugs, the headache powders are the most widely used."

Other Articles to be Announced Later

If you can not secure these issues from your dealer, they will be mailed to you on receipt of price, which may be sent in the form of stamps. Address P. F. COLLIER & SON, 420 West Thirteenth Street, New York City

NEWSDEALERS
EVERYWHERE

Collier's
THE NATIONAL WEEKLY

TEN CENTS
PER COPY

90

The Most Durable and Economical Stove Polish

It will not cake on the iron; it will not burn red; it will not stain the hands; it will not harden, and is not affected by heat, cold, age or climate. When moisture is added, the last particle can be used. Three thousand tons sold yearly. Many have tried other kinds said to be just as good, only to come back to the reliable RISING SUN STOVE POLISH, because

IT GIVES THE SHINE THAT LASTS

IT IS APPLIED AND POLISHED WITH A BRUSH

IN PASTE FORM

SUN PASTE STOVE POLISH

Morse Brothers, Proprietors • • • Canton, Mass., U. S. A.

The Little Joys of Every Day

What a charming success is a meal with Nabisco Sugar Wafers—little confections and yet their presence means so much. What a plain, matter-of-fact, prosaic failure is that same meal without

NABISCO

Those delightful dessert confections that exhilarate the palate and caress the tongue—helpful allies not only for the great events, but for the little joys of every day. What would a dinner be without Nabisco!

In ten and twenty-five cent tins.

FESTINO—A confection which looks like an almond nut, but is really a deliciously piquant morsel of goodness.

NATIONAL BISCUIT COMPANY

III Potpourri

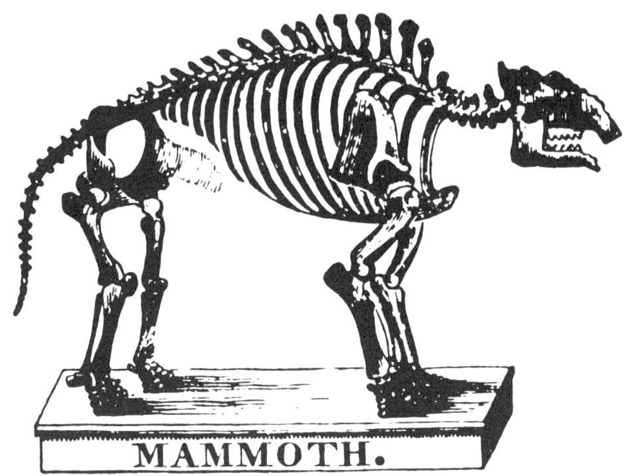

Philadelphia Museum,

IN THE UPPER PART OF THE

ARCADE,

CHESNUT STREET, (ABOVE SIXTH.)

OPEN thoughout the day, and ILLUMINATED every evening.

Admittance 25 Cents.

This Museum is the oldest and largest establishment in the United States, and contains immense collections of the Animal and Mineral kingdoms of nature, from all parts of the world. These are all beautifully arranged, so as to enable the visitor to study the objects with the greatest advantage. The collection of implements and ornaments of our aboriginal tribes is very extensive and interesting, and the Cabinet of Antiquities, and Artificial Curiosities, is not less worthy of attention. In addition to the ordinary attractions of a Museum, there is in this a very large collection of the Portraits of American Statesmen and Warriors of the Revolution, and of the most distinguished scientific men of Europe and America.

The Founder, C. W. Peale, desirous of securing the Museum permanently in this city, obtained an act of Incorporation, by which the stability of the Institution is insured. The act of Incorporation secures the use of the Museum in perpetuity to the city, and authorizes the Stockholders to appoint annually five trustees, who meet quarterly to regulate the business of the Institution. Nothing can be removed from the Institution under a penalty, and forfeiture of double the value of the thing removed; hence donations may be made with certainty on the part of the donors, that the articles placed in the Museum will always remain for the public good.

(1829)

94

NEWS! NEWS!!

A ARON O LIVER, *Poſt-Rider,*

W ISHES to inform the Public, that he has extended his Route ; and that he now rides thro' the towns of *Troy, Pittſtown, Hooſick, Ma-pletown,* part of *Bennington* and *Shaftſbury, Peters-burgh, Stephentown, Greenbuſh* and *Schodack.*

All commands in his line will be re-ceived with thanks, and executed with punctuality.

He returns his ſincere thanks to his former cuſtomers ; and intends, by unabated diligence, to merit a continuance of their favours.

> *O'er ruggid hills, aud vallies wide,*
> *He never yet has fail'd to trudge it :*
> *As ſteady as the flowing tide,*
> *He hands about the* N ORTHERN B UDGET.

June 18, 1799.

H. DICKSON,
HATS, CAPS & FURS,
No. 60 STATE STREET, ALBANY.

(1855)

"DON'T-SNORE"
U. S. Patent
Positively prevents snoring and mouth breathing: keeps the nostrils open and clear, allows normal breathing through the nose, adjusted in a moment, comfortable, convenient. Gold filled. One Dollar. postpaid. If unsatisfactory after 30 days' trial money refunded upon return of "Don't-Snore,"
SIMPLE DEVICE SALES CO.
Box 503   LEESBURG, VA.

(1913)

EDISON'S
POLYFORM
CURES
RHEUMATISM,
NEURALGIA,
SCIATICA,
And all Nervous Pains.
PREPARED BY THE
Menlo Park Manufacturing Co., New York.
PRICE, $1.00—SOLD BY ALL DRUGGISTS.
(1880)

FROG IN YOUR THROAT
10¢
ALL
DRUGGISTS
Stops
that
tickle!
Greatest Cough & Voice Lozenge on Earth

(1917)

WILL KILL AT 100 YARDS
RIFLE BORE
2.2 CALIBRE 7 SHOT TRY IT
ONLY $1.00
This Advertisement Will Not Appear Again.

The Saxon Importing Co., agrees to send by express to any of our readers an extra fine full Nickel Plated 7 shot, 22 calibre, 5 3-4 in. long Revolver upon SENDING THEM the following CERTIFICATE and $1.00 to pay expenses of advertising and packing; or send them $1.00 and 6 three cent stamps (18c.) and they will send it by mail post-paid. To be fancy engraved, it will cost 25 cents extra. Remember this Revolver will not be furnished at above price unless accompanied by this Certificate.

CERTIFICATE.—Saxon Importing Co., enclosed find amount as above required to pay for an extra fine Nickel Plated 7 Shot, 22 calibre, 5 3-4 in. long Revolver, and I agree upon receipt of said Revolver to show it and your Catalogues to my friends. Address,
SAXON IMPORTING CO., 116 Chambers St., New York.

(1882)

Imported Absolutely !!

Only the best and purest malt vinegar—made in our own breweries, on the banks of the River Stour, Worcestershire, England—is used.

It takes over two years of careful preparation and ageing to produce the full, rich, mellow flavour

A good wine cannot be made in a day—neither can Holbrook's Sauce.

"It is better to use no sauce at all than a sauce that is not Holbrook's."

HOLBROOK'S WORCESTERSHIRE SAUCE

(1913)

The Noyes Reading Machine removes that embargo on reading— the task of holding up a heavy book by the hour—and reduces the labor of reading to simply moving the eyes from line to line. It is a boon to invalids, a joy to well people, and invaluable for children in school, removing the cause of round shoulders, placing the book where it should be. It handles heavy books as easily as light ones, and holds them open at any angle or in any position. The book is held by the covers, the leaves are held open with a Leaf-Holder, which by a touch can be removed or replaced. A clamp attaches it to a table or desk. An extension arm attaches to chairs book-cases, diction-ary holders, etc. Special introductory prices: Reading Machine with Leaf-Holder and Clamp complete, $1.00 Extension Arm with Attachments, $1.00. Sent post paid on receipt of price
Address L. W. NOYES, the Maker of Dictionary Holders, Chicago. Cut this off and show the above to your friends. Get five to send with you and you shall have yours free. Six for $5.00. This offer is not good unless accepted at once.

(1883)

SAUER'S FLAVORING EXTRACTS
Leading European and American chemists have placed 14 highest awards on Sauer's Flavoring Extracts, for their purity, strength, and fine flavor. Insist upon Sauer's (pronounced Sour's) Flavoring Extracts, they cost no more than cheap imitations. Sold in 10 and 25c. sizes everywhere. Be sure your grocer sends Sauer's

(1915)

TO KNOW

how to clothe the

CHILDREN

BOYS,

GIRLS,

BABIES

In the latest styles and best manner at the least trouble and expense, send for the

Liliputian Bazaar

CATALOGUE

"OUR PERFECT." Which we mail free.

Our "Perfect" waists are incomparably the best in the world. They support the clothing directly from the shoulder, and will be found indispensable for their comfort and hygienic value to a growing child. We send them for trial subject to return for refund of money if not satisfactory.

Everything for Children's wear from Hats to Shoes.

BEST & CO. 60 W. 23d Street, Bet. 5th & 6th Aves. N. Y.

(1883)

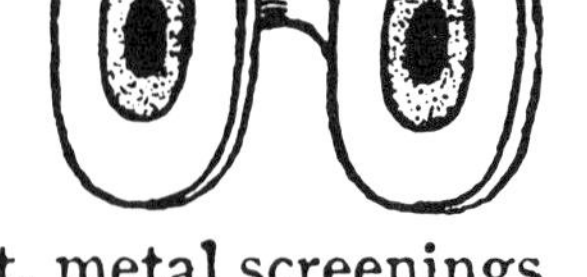

NASAL SHIELD
FOR HAY FEVER

The Carence Nasal Shield has been successfully used for years to prevent and relieve hay fever and all inflammations from dust, metal screenings and other irritations. PROMPT RELIEF.

Price $5.00. Write for Booklet.

NASAL SHIELD CO., 1724 Wabash Ave., Kansas City, Mo.

(1916)

MEDINA'S LISBON WAVE.

Suitable for all ages. Warranted to withstand dampness. Prices for small sizes, **$10** and **$12**; medium size, **$15**; large, **$18**; with straight or wavy back hair. Small sizes, without back hair, $5 to **$10.**

LADIES' and GENTS' WIGS from $10 up.

On receipt of sample shade, *will forward goods by mail to any part of the U. S. for approval, before the price is paid.* Send for circular to

JOHN MEDINA,
Paris Hair Store,
463 Washington Street, Boston, Mass.

(1884)

DISFIGURING Humors, Humiliating Eruptions, Itching Tortures, Scrofula, Salt Rheum, and Infantile Humors cured by the CUTICURA REMEDIES.

CUTICURA RESOLVENT, the new blood purifier, cleanses the blood and perspiration of impurities and poisonous elements, and thus removes the *cause*.

CUTICURA, the great Skin Cure, instantly allays Itching and Inflammation, clears the Skin and Scalp, heals Ulcers and Sores, and restores the Hair.

CUTICURA SOAP, an exquisite Skin Beautifier and Toilet Requisite, prepared from CUTICURA, is indispensable in treating Skin Diseases, Baby Humors, Skin Blemishes, Sunburn, and Greasy Skin.

CUTICURA REMEDIES are absolutely pure, and the only infallible Blood Purifiers and Skin Beautifiers.

Sold everywhere. Price, Cuticura, 50 cents; Soap, 25 cents; Resolvent, $1.

POTTER DRUG AND CHEMICAL CO., BOSTON, MASS.

(1884)

TAPE-WORM Expelled ALIVE in 60 minutes

with he'd, or no charge. Send 2c. stamp for Pamphlet.
Dr. M. Ney Smith, Specialist. 1011 Olive st., St. Louis, Mo.

(1894)

THE CANFIELD

Patent, "Elastic Seamless"

DRESS SHIELDS

are waterproof, absorbent, odorless, strong, yet soft as kid, do not wrinkle, chafe or rip, are easily shaped to the garment and only *seamless* shield made. This is a recent American invention and the sales are already double that of any other Dress Protector made in Europe or United States. These goods are protected by patents and trade marks all over the world.

Beware of imitations. All genuine goods bear the trade mark shown above.

The Canfield Rubber Co., Middletown, Conn.

(1884)

106

ONLY FOR MOTH PATCHES,

FRECKLES and TAN,

Use **Perry's Moth and Freckle Lotion.** It is reliable

FOR PIMPLES ON THE FACE,

Blackheads, and Fleshworms.

Ask your druggist for PERRY'S COMEDONE and Pimple Remedy, the infallible skin medicine. Send for circular. **Brent Good & Co., 57** Murray Street, New York.

(1884)

CURES WITHOUT DRUGS

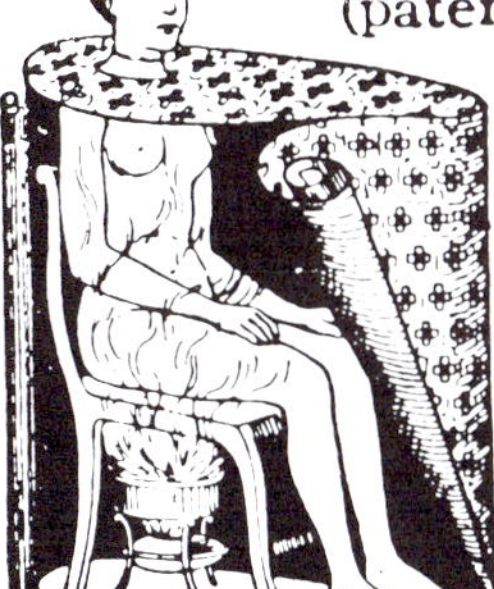

Every home should have our New Improved Thermal Vapor Bath Cabinet (patented.) It gives a hot vapor bath which forces all impurities from the system by natural action of the pores of the skin. Immediate relief guaranteed in worst forms of **Rheumatism, Neuralgia, La Grippe, Gout, Female Complaints, Insomnia; all Blood, Skin, Nerve and Kidney Diseases; reduces Surplus Flesh. One bath cures the worst cold.**

Unequaled for general bathing purposes. Folds up when not in use. Ladies should have our **Complexion Steamer,** used in conjunction with Cabinet. Invaluable for the successful treatment of Asthma and Catarrh. **Clears the skin, removes pimples, blemishes and salt rheum;** gives a soft, velvety complexion.

FREE Descriptive book and testimonials to all who write. **SPECIAL INDUCEMENTS to AGENTS.** MOLLENKOPP & McCREERY, 224 Summit St., TOLEDO, OHIO.

(1898)

(1884)

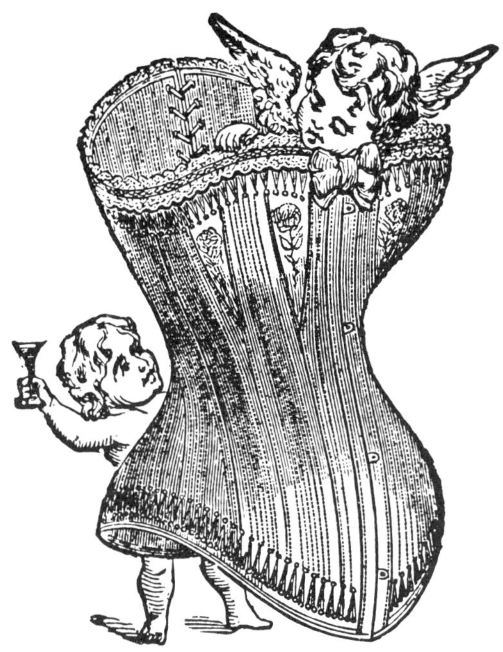

THINGS TO REMEMBER.

Warner Bros. Corsets are boned with **Coraline,** which is superior to Horn or Whalebone.

Coraline is not Cotton, Hemp, Jute, Tampico, or Mexican Grass.

Coraline contains no Starch or other sizing.

Coraline is used in no goods except those sold by WARNER BROS.

The genuine **Coraline** Corsets give honest value and perfect satisfaction.

Imitations are a fraud, and dear at any price.

Coraline is used in the following popular styles: **Health, Nursing, Coraline, Flexible Hip, Abdominal** and **Misses' Corsets.**

FOR SALE BY LEADING MERCHANTS EVERYWHERE.

Be sure our name is on the box.

WARNER BROS.,

353 BROADWAY,   NEW YORK

(1884)

MARK TWAIN'S NEW WORK,
"ADVENTURES OF
HUCKLEBERRY FINN"
(Tom Sawyer's Comrade.)
APPEARS FEBRUARY 18th
Prospectuses now ready.
Fine Heliotype of the
author in each book.
Agents wanted. Splendid Terms!
CHARLES L. WEBSTER & CO.
Publishers,
658 BROADWAY, NEW YORK CITY.

(1885)

EAT BICYCLES
SAVE MONEY
Without Charge.
A.W. GUMP
& CO.,
Dayton, O.
will send you a
list of new and
second-hand Bicycles, showing a saving of
from $20.00 to $50.00, or for 10 cents they will
send you a Candy Bicycle Transparency, good
to eat but better to hang in your window.

(1894)

MADAME DEAN'S SPINAL SUPPORTING CORSETS.

They support the **Spine**, **relieve** the muscles of the back, **brace the shoulders** in a natural and easy manner, imparting **graceful carriage** to the wearer without discomfort, **expanding the chest**, thereby giving **full action to the lungs**, and **health** and **comfort** to the body. Take the place of the ORDINARY CORSET in every respect, and are made of fine Coutil, in the best manner, in various styles and sold by agents everywhere at **popular prices**. **Mrs. Wm. Papes**, Keota, Iowa, says:—I have been an invalid for six years, have travelled extensively for health, yet never received as much benefit as I have in a few weeks wear, of your MADAME, DEAN'S CORSET. I am gaining strength all the time, and could not do without it. It has proven to me a *godsend*.

FREE Our new book entitled: "Dress Reform for Ladies" with elegant wood engraving and Biography of **Worth**, the **King of Fashion**, Paris; also our **New Illustrated Catalogue** sent **free** to any address on receipt of two 2-cent stamps to pay postage and packing.

AGENTS WANTED for these **celebrated Corsets**. No experience required. Four orders per day give the agent **$150 monthly**. Our agents report from four to twenty sales daily. **$3.00** Outfit Free. Send for terms and full particulars. **SCHIELE & CO., 390 Broadway, New York.**

(1885)

"DRINK FAIR, BETSEY, WOTEVER YOU DO."
Martin Chuzzlewit.

TEA CLUB ORDERS.

We have made a specialty for six years of *giving away* as Premiums, to those who get up clubs for our goods. *Dinner and Tea Sets, Gold Band Sets, Silverware, etc.* Teas of all kinds, from 30 to 75 cents per pound. We **do** a very large Tea and Coffee business, besides sending out from 60 to 90 **CLUB ORDERS** each day. **SILVER-PLATED CASTERS** as Premiums with **$5, $7** and **$10** orders. **WHITE TEA SETS** with **$10** orders. **DECORATED TEA SETS** with **$13. GOLD BAND** or **MOSS ROSE SETS** of **44 pieces,** or **DINNER SETS** of **112 pieces,** with **$20** orders, and a **Host** of other Premiums. Send us postal and mention this paper, and we will send you full Price and **Illustrated Premium List.** Freight charges average 75 cents per 100 pounds to points West.

GREAT LONDON TEA CO.,
801 Washington Street, Boston, Mass.

(1885)

112

The "TASKER"
SKATING SHOE.
Sent to any part of the United States for $3.00
Manufactured by
H. & F. H. TASKER
991 AND 993 Fulton Street,
Near St. James Place,
BROOKLYN, N. Y.
Send for Descriptive Catalogue.

(1885)

Holmes & Co.
JERSEY BATHING SUITS
READERS IN VICINITY OF BOSTON CALL & EXAMINE.
TAKE ELEVATOR SEND STAMP FOR CATALOGUE
109 Kingston St
BOSTON MASS.
FULL TIGHTS FOR BATHING
ALLEN PRINT

(1886)

POCKET
DRINKING CUP
(Silver plated.)
Folds together and goes
in case size of watch.
50c. each; 3 for $1.25;
$4 per doz. to Agents.
Connecticut Novelty Co.,
Meriden, Conn.

(1886)

AVOID BULK SODA
Bad Soda Spoils Good Flour.
Pure Soda—the Best Soda, comes
only in PACKAGES
Bearing Trade Mark: ARM and HAMMER.
It costs no more than inferior package Soda
—never spoils the flour—always keeps soft.
Beware of Imitation trade marks and labels,
and INSIST ON PACKAGES
bearing these words—
ARM & HAMMER
CHURCH & CO'S
SODA
NEW YORK.
ARM & HAMMER SODA
MADE ONLY BY
CHURCH & CO. NEW YORK.
SOLD BY GROCERS EVERYWHERE.
Write for Arm and Hammer Book of Valuable Recipes—FREE.

(1888)

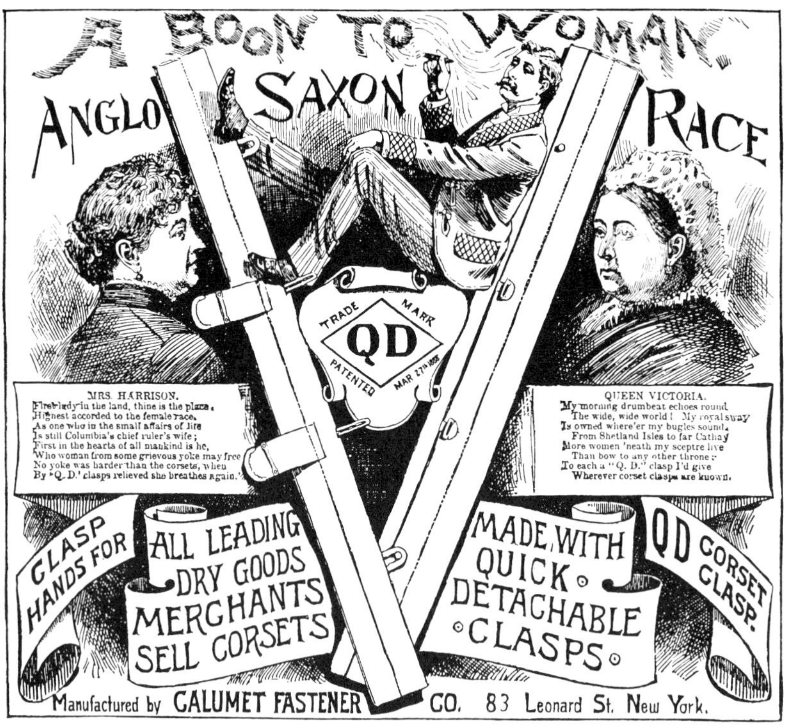

(1886)

History made
LIBERTY BELL
honored and loved.

Sweetness and purity of tone have made

THE NEW DEPARTURE BICYCLE BELLS

widely known and universally appreciated.
The acme of excellence. The ideal of perfection.

THE NEW DEPARTURE BELL CO., 16 Main St., Bristol, Conn.

(1897)

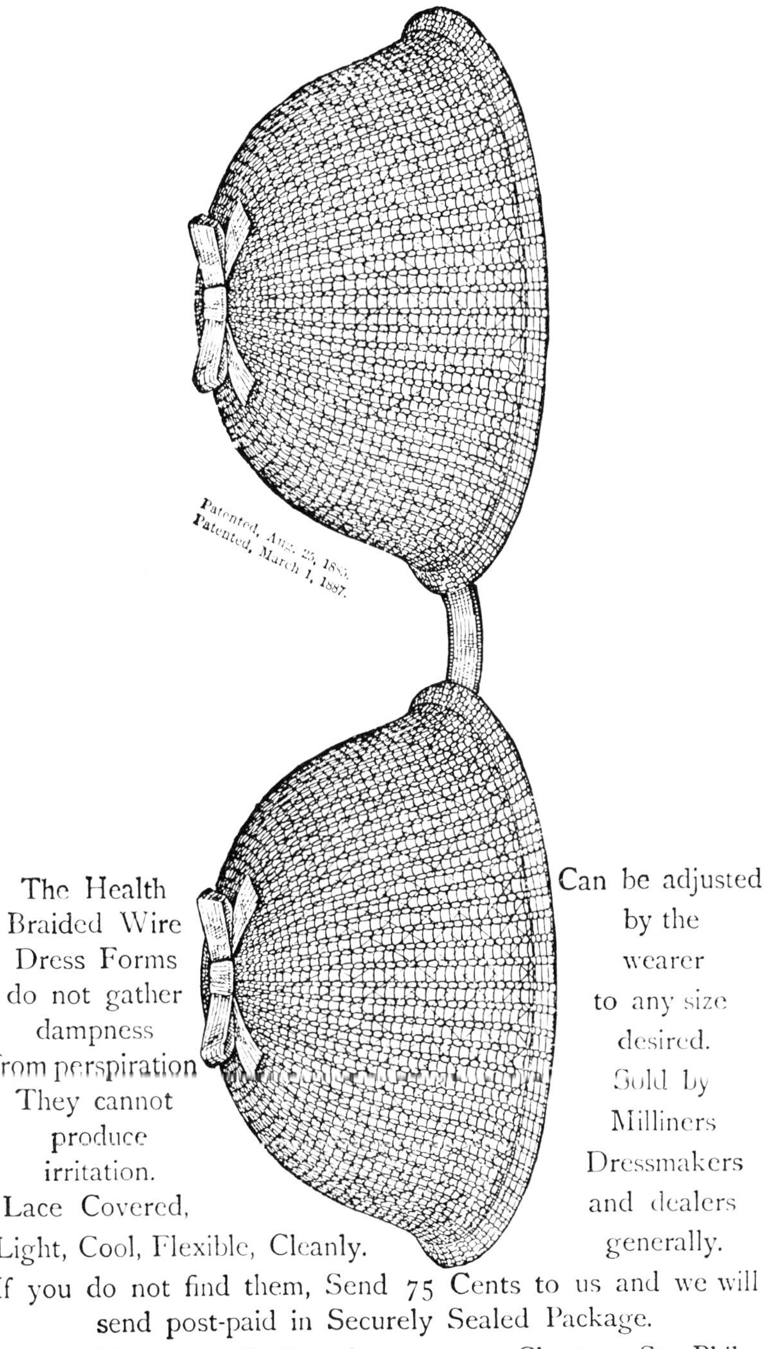

The Health Braided Wire Dress Forms do not gather dampness from perspiration They cannot produce irritation. Lace Covered, Light, Cool, Flexible, Cleanly. Can be adjusted by the wearer to any size desired. Sold by Milliners Dressmakers and dealers generally.

If you do not find them, Send 75 Cents to us and we will send post-paid in Securely Sealed Package.

Stokes, Thompson & Co., Agents, 235 Chestnut St., Phila.

Price Lists to Dealers.

A Sample will be sent to any Milliner or Dressmaker sending their Business Card and 60c.

(1887)

117

A beautiful work of 150 pages, Colored Plate, and 1000 illustrations, with descriptions of the best Flowers and Vegetables, prices of Seeds and Plants, and how to grow them. Printed in English and German. Price only 10 cents, which may be deducted from first order.

It tells what you want for the garden, and how to get it instead of running to the grocery at the last moment to buy whatever seeds happen to be left over, meeting with disappointment after weeks of waiting.

BUY ONLY VICK'S SEEDS AT HEADQUARTERS.

VICK'S ILLUSTRATED MONTHLY MAGAZINE, 32 pages, a Colored Plate in every number, and many fine engravings. Price, $1.25 a year; Five Copies for $5. Specimen numbers 10 cents; 3 trial copies 25 cents. We will send to any address Vick's Magazine and any one of the following publications at the prices named below —really two magazines at the price of one—Century, $4.50; Harper's Monthly, $4.00; St. Nicholas, $3.50; Good Cheer, $1.25; Illustrated Christian Weekly, $3.00; **or Wide Awake, Good Cheer, and Vick's Magazine for $3.00.**

VICK'S FLOWER AND VEGETABLE GARDEN, 210 pages, Six Colored Plates, nearly 1000 Engravings, $1.25, in elegant cloth covers.

JAMES VICK, Rochester, N. Y.

(188·8)

118

BALL-POINTED PENS.

(H. Hewitt's Patent—America, 295,395; Britain, 429.)

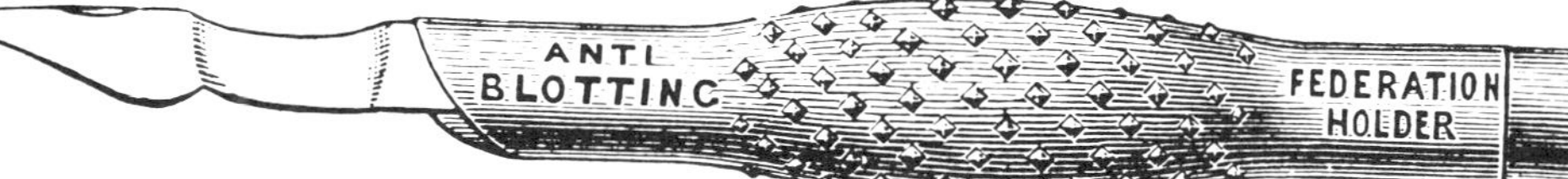

The most important improvement in Steel Pens since first introduced. For writing in every position—never scratch nor spurt—hold more ink and last longer. Seven sorts, suitable for ledger, bold, rapid, or professional writing. Price, **$1.20** and **$1.50** per gross. *Buy an assorted sample box for* **25** *cents, and choose a pen to suit your hand.*

THE "FEDERATION HOLDERS" NOT ONLY PREVENT THE PEN FROM BLOTTING, BUT GIVE A FIRM AND COMFORTABLE GRIP. PRICE 5, 15 & 20 CENTS. TO BE HAD OF ALL STATIONERS.

(1888)

ALLCOCK'S POROUS PLASTERS,
THE
STANDARD PLASTERS OF THE WORLD
ARE
USED AND PREFERRED BY ALL.

(1888)

120

What's all this Fuss about a Nail?

Because every man who owns a horse knows that the animal is of no value or use un-less it has sound feet, and soundness depends very largely on the nail used in shoeing. Some nails SPLIT when driven into the hard hoof, one point coming out where it should, to be clenched, the other going into the tender part of the foot, causing either permanent lameness or lockjaw, followed by death. Such cases are frequent and can be easily referred to. THE PUTNAM NAIL cannot SPLIT, SLIVER or BREAK. It is Hot-Forged and Hammer-Pointed, and is the only Horse-Shoe Nail made by machinery that is exactly like an old-fashioned hand-made nail. When your horse is shod do not let the blacksmith use a CHEAP NAIL; it may RUIN YOUR HORSE. Insist on the PUTNAM.

THE PUTNAM NAILS are made in various sizes to meet every requirement:—**The Government Standard**—Regular Nail; **Turf Nail**—A light Nail for race-horses; **City Head**—For hand-made shoes; **Counters**—Long heads for railroad and special shoes.

For sale by all dealers in Horse-Shoe Nails. Samples free by mail. *Mention The Youth's Companion.*

THE PUTNAM NAIL CO., Neponset P. O., Boston, Mass.

(1889)

EDISON ⚡ LAMPS

For Decorative, Surgical, Dental, poses. From ⅕ er. From 2½ Catalogue on

Experimental, and other pur to 36 candle pow to 40 volts. application.

EDISON LAMP CO.

Harrison,   N. J.

(1889)

This Wonderful Improved
SAW MACHINE

is warranted to saw a **2-foot log in three minutes,** and **more** cord wood or logs of any size in a day than **two men** can chop or saw the old way. Every Farmer and Lumberman needs one. **ACENTS WANTED**—Circular and terms Free. Address **FARMER'S MANUFACTURING CO.,** 178 Elm Street, Cincinnati, O.

(1881)

If you must part with $100
WHEN BUYING A WRITING MACHINE PAY
$35 for "The Chicago"
AND GIVE $65.00 AWAY.
You will be better satisfied with your investment than
if you put the whole sum into some other typewriter.
CHICAGO WRITING MACHINE CO.
The Chicago.
Pat'd Sep 17 1889 Feb 10, 1891 Mar 3 1892.

USE
PEARL TOP LAMP
THE BEST CHIMNEYS
MADE ONLY BY IN THE WORLD
GEO. A. MACBETH & CO. PITTSBURGH, PA.

(1889)

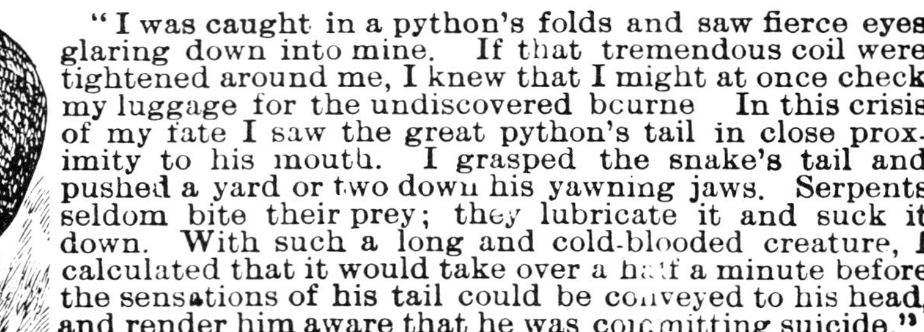

"I was caught in a python's folds and saw fierce eyes glaring down into mine. If that tremendous coil were tightened around me, I knew that I might at once check my luggage for the undiscovered bourne. In this crisis of my fate I saw the great python's tail in close proximity to his mouth. I grasped the snake's tail and pushed a yard or two down his yawning jaws. Serpents seldom bite their prey; they lubricate it and suck it down. With such a long and cold-blooded creature, I calculated that it would take over a half a minute before the sensations of his tail could be conveyed to his head, and render him aware that he was committing suicide."

NEW BOOK FOR BOYS, EXCITING AS MUNCHAUSEN.

Hairbreadth Escapes of
MAJOR MENDAX.

By F. BLAKE CROFTON. His perilous encounters, startling adventures and daring exploits with Indians, Cannibals, Wild Beast, Serpents, Balloons, Geysers, etc., all over the World, in the bowels of the earth and above the Clouds, *a personal narrative. Spirited Illustrations* by Bennett. **225** pages. **Cloth, elegant, $2.00.** Press critics say: *"Irresistibly comic."*—CHRISTIAN WORLD. *"Bold but humorous."*—PUBLIC OPINION. *"Munchausen never imagined greater marvels."*—NEWS. *"Beats everything of its kind."*—GAZETTE. *For sale by all Booksellers,* or mailed on receipt of price. HUBBARD BROS., Pubs., 723 Chestnut St., Philada.

(1889)

WE MANUFACTURE THE GREATEST VARIETY OF VEHICLES IN THE WORLD.
IF NOT SOLD BY YOUR DEALER WRITE
Copyrighted
THE FAMOUS FOUR HUNDRED" BUCKBOARD
MADE ONLY BY
THE BIDDLE & SMART CO.
ESTABLISHED 1870.
AMESBURY, MASS. U.S.A.
LONDON ENG
W. E. BIDDLE, PREST. & TREAS.
W. W. SMART, V. PREST & SUPT.
M. D. F. STEERE, V. PREST.
FRANK STINSON, SECTY.
(1890)

125

HERRING'S SAFES

For Residences.

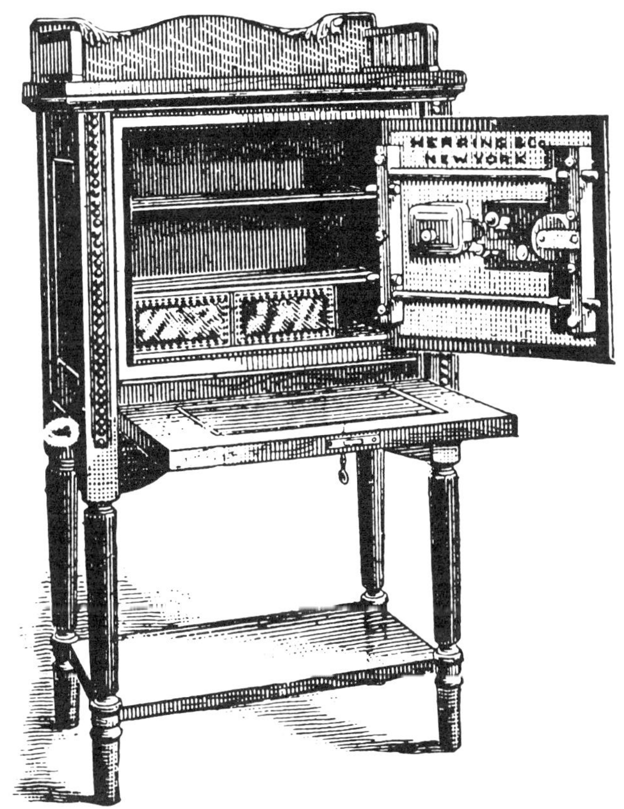

HERRING & CO.,

Nos. 251 & 252 BROADWAY, NEW YORK.

(1891)

EAR CAP.

For remedying Prominent Ears, Preventing Disfigurement in after life.

In all sizes.

Send measure around head, just above ears; also from bottom of lobe of ear over head to bottom of other ear, not under chin. Price $1.25.

BEST & CO.

60 & 62 West 23d Street, N. Y.

(1892)

(1895)

LET ME MAKE YOU A NEW FACE. I CAN DO IT.
I have been doing it for 20 years.

WILL YOUR FACE STAND CLOSE INSPECTION? Get the hand-mirror. Take a good look at yourself. Have you tried WOODBURY'S FACIAL SOAP?

YOUR COMPLEXION IS BAD. It has cost you much humiliation. It will continue to do so unless you use WOODBURY'S FACIAL SOAP. At druggists', or by mail, 50c.

I WILL PUT A FACE ON YOU. A good face, a good scalp, a good complexion. I will do the most of it with WOODBURY'S FACIAL SOAP. At druggists', or by mail, 50c.

20 YEARS' EXPERIENCE. Just think, every day for over seven thousand days I have been at work on sickly complexions, eruptive faces and scalps, removing pimples, scars and disfigurements of every description. I have made more valuable discoveries than any other Dermatologist.

HAVE YOU EVER been tempted to look beautiful? WOODBURY'S FACIAL SOAP will do what your looking-glass has often said could not be done. It is a skin beautifier. Send for book and sample.

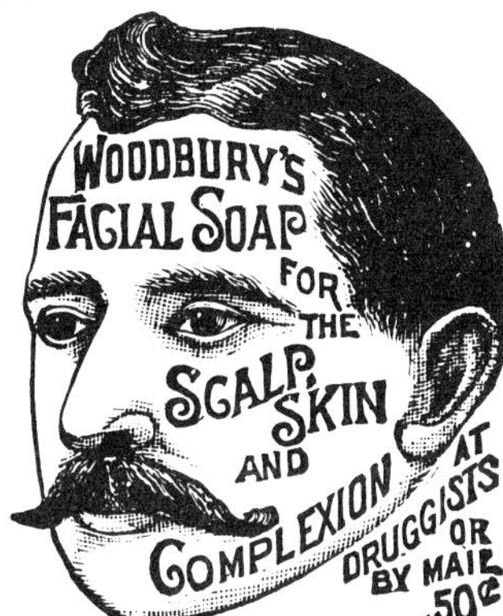

I CAN'T take the spots off a frog. Soap was not invented for that purpose, but WOODBURY'S FACIAL SOAP will make the human skin most beautiful to look upon. At druggists', or by mail, 50c.

CONSTIPATION, its cure and treatment; not a physic. Send for book.

ARSENIC, its effects on the skin and the blood. Read the article in book.

FACE STEAMING, the latest fad. Can be used at home. Price $5. Send for book.

THAT NERVOUS FEELING one has when riding in the cars is indicative of trouble. Send for 145-page book.

IF YOU COULD SEE yourself as others see you, you would go at once to Dermatologist JOHN H. WOODBURY, 125 West 42d street.

WRINKLES are banished by the latest improved method.

DO THE PUBLIC know a good thing when they see it? Not always. They know a good thing when they try it. Perhaps there are some who have not tried WOODBURY'S FACIAL SOAP. I want to know who and where they are. I advertise for that purpose.

SPOTTED FACES, birthmarks. India ink, freckles, etc. People running about with any of the above labels will please express themselves or write to JOHN H. WOODBURY, Dermatologist, 125 West 42d street.

DON'T THROW YOUR FACE AWAY. No matter if you are tired of it. Don't let it go until you have read DR. WOODBURY'S Book or called upon him.

YOUR BREATH IS TERRIBLE. I think you have Catarrh or dropping of the mucus matter in your throat. For the sake of others who sit beside you, call or write Dermatologist JOHN H. WOODBURY, 125 West 42d street, N. Y. City.

THE BEARD LINE. If the hair is above the beard line or between the eyes, it can be permanently removed.

FOR THE SAKE of the one who sits beside you in the car get those pimples off your face. Send 10c. for 145-page Book and sample cake of soap.

CORPULENCY Pills reduce flesh 10 pounds per month, with diet. Send for Book.

CATARRH.—Read the chapter on it in the book published by JOHN H. WOODBURY.

THE NEW FACIAL INSTRUMENT is applicable to all fleshy parts of the body, and should be on the toilet table of every lady and gentleman.

SUPERFLUOUS HAIR on the female face looks badly and makes the patient bashful.

THE RED AND PURPLE VEINS on your nose will no longer show if treated by Dermatologist JOHN H. WOODBURY, 125 West 42d street, New York City.

YOU ARE NERVOUS. It is noticeable. You may not think so, but it is a fact. Read the book.

YOUR EYES AND CHEEKS ARE SUNKEN IN. In fact your general appearance indicates Nervous Debility.

A BIG HEAD or a small head with a diseased scalp is unnecessary.

UNTIMELY GRAYNESS is indicative of a diseased condition of the scalp. Send 10c. for 145-page book.

THE GROWTH OF YOUR MUSTACHE can be increased by the latest method.

"FRECKLES," "MOTH-PATCHES" and all other skin blemishes removed.

THE DANDRUFF on your shoulders is indicative of a diseased scalp. It is noticeable and filthy. Read the book of JOHN H. WOODBURY, Dermatologist.

THE PITTINGS on your face I am sure I can erase if you my place will trace.

NO SURGICAL OPERATION is needed to remove that hideous birthmark.

IF YOUR EYEBROWS are thick and run together I would advise you to seek the office of JOHN H. WOODBURY.

THAT RED ROUGHNESS of your skin is incipient Eczema. Stop it at once.

READ THE CHAPTER on Scars, Wrinkles and Pittings in Book by JOHN H. WOODBURY, Dermatologist.

THIN FACES ROUNDED, hard lines softened, wrinkles banished and blemishes eradicated.

THOSE HAIRLESS SPOTS on your scalp is a disease called Alopesia, or falling of the hair. It can be cured.

AGE, ILLNESS AND CARE cause wrinkles. Dermatologist JOHN H. WOODBURY removes them.

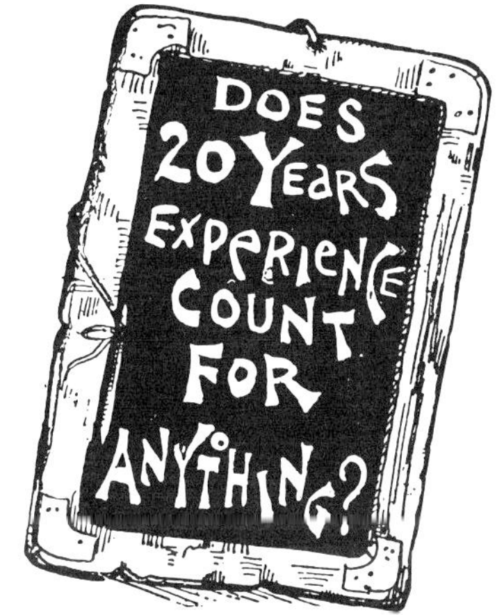

IF YOUR EYEBROWS were a little thicker you would be much prettier. It can be done.

YOUR EARS are ill-shaped. They stand out too far from the head.

YOUR CHEEKS are sunken in. Don't use plumpers, but read the article on Facial Development by JOHN H. WOODBURY, Dermatologist.

SUPERFLUOUS HAIR permanently removed by the electric needle, never to return again.

WARTS AND PIMPLES on the Scalp, very annoying to ladies, successfully removed without the knife.

A LEAN FACE may be made plump and pleasing.

"BEAUTY IS BUT SKIN DEEP." In other words, with a blemished skin there can be no beauty.

A RED NOSE IS NOT always a sign of drink.

A Sample Cake of Soap and 145-page Book sent sealed for 10c., Illustrated, on Skin, Scalp, Nervous and Blood Diseases.

JOHN H. WOODBURY, Dermatologist, 125 W. 42d St., New York City.
CONSULTATION FREE, AT OFFICE OR BY LETTER.   ESTABLISHED 1870.

(1892)

129

WE WANT YOU to try **Golden Sceptre.** All the talk in the world will not convince you so quickly as a trial that it is almost **PERFECTION.** We will send on receipt of **10c.** a sample to any address. 1 lb., $1.30, 1-4 lb., 40 cts., postage paid. Send for Catalogue giving list of dealers who handle our goods, **SURBRUG, 159 Fulton St., N. Y. City.**

(1893)

TRADE MARK
SURE DEATH
It Kills
Every Kind
of Vermin
RATS, MICE.
ROACHES
BUGS
and every house-
hold pest exter-
minated by
Stearns' ELECTRIC
RAT AND ROACH PASTE
SURE, SAFE, INSTANT.
At all Druggists and Grocers. 25 cents per box.

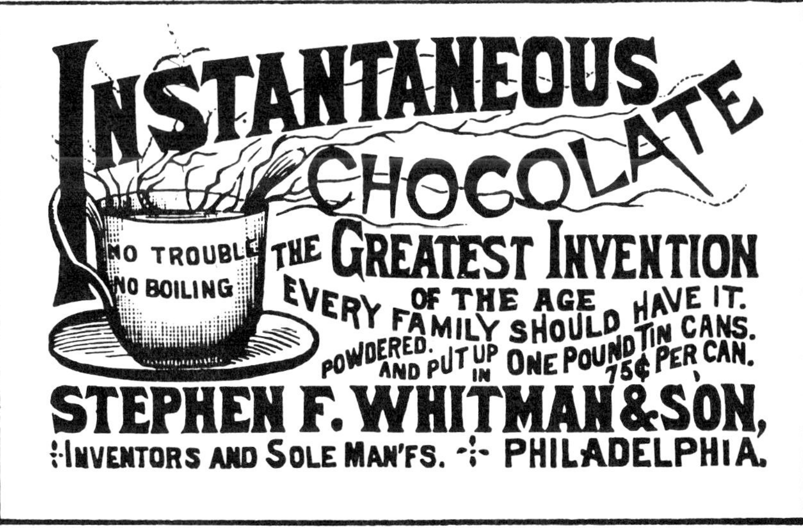

INSTANTANEOUS
CHOCOLATE
NO TROUBLE
NO BOILING
THE GREATEST INVENTION
OF THE AGE
EVERY FAMILY SHOULD HAVE IT.
POWDERED.
AND PUT UP IN ONE POUND TIN CANS.
75¢ PER CAN.
STEPHEN F. WHITMAN & SON,
INVENTORS AND SOLE MAN'FS. PHILADELPHIA.

(1893)

IN BUILDING A HOUSE

it is well to know that the difference between the Standard Porcelain-lined Bath Tubs and other kinds is that the Standard baths are absolutely pure inside, and as beautiful as you please without.

Doctors say they are sanitary; housekeepers say they are always clean; builders say they are the most economical, because the most durable, and that, while the choice in price is great, the inside is always the same. They are found in all the best houses and leading hotels. Illustrated Catalogue free.

STANDARD M'F'G CO., Box 1028 J, Pittsburgh, Pa.

(1892)

Stearns Ball-Bearing Mower.

The bearings are micrometer-gauged balls, revolving between accurately adjusted hardened ground steel cones and cups.

For sale by Hardware Dealers generally. Descriptive circular and prices on application.

E. C. STEARNS & CO., SYRACUSE, N. Y.

(1898)

Coat and Vest to Order
in Clay's Diagonals $12 & $15.

These goods are soft finished and will not gloss. We will give you a written guarantee that they are foreign goods. Leave your order for one of our $18.00 Spring overcoats. They can't be beaten. We have the largest line of trouserings at $5 in this country.

TAKE NOTICE.

We have recently added a new department to our establishment, our object being to sell cloth by the yard on the smallest margin possible. With that end in view, we are receiving cloth from the largest mills in the world. All our goods are shrunk and ready for use.

Samples and self-measurement guide forwarded by mail free of charge.

Representatives wanted in every state in the Union to take orders for our stylish garments, made to order.

JACOBS BROTHERS,
229 Broadway (Opp. Post-Office).
152 & 154 Bowery (Cor. Broome St.).

(1892)

PRICE $1.00
WATCH POCKET LAMP
AND 1,000 LIGHTS, $1.00.
100,000 IN USE. SENT TO ALL
PARTS OF THE U. S., PREPAID, FOR
$1.00.
For Sale by the Cigar Trade.
WATCH POCKET LAMP
PAT JUNE 23 JULY 21, 9
NEW YORK
FOLMER & SCHWING MFG CO
FOLMER & SCHWING
MANUFACTURING CO.,
Manufacturers of Gas Fixtures, Etc.,
271 Canal Street, NEW YORK.

(1893)

Your Money Back If You Want It.
$2.74 $1.84
Double-breasted Suit of good Navy Blue Cheviot, with extra pants, cap, and good fast black stockings. 4 to 14 years. $2.74 or
$3.00 post-paid.
Sailor Suit good navy blue flannel with extra pants, cap, cord, whistle, and good fast black stockings. 4 to 12 years. $1.84 or
$2.00 post-paid.
Shaughnessy Bros., 7th Ave. and 130th St., NEW YORK.

(1895)

$280 earned in 6 days by the "**INVESTOR**" for its owner; the best paying slot machine ever invented. Price $50.00. Send for catalogue "Nickel Tickler," Card "3 for 1," "Pencil Printing," "Dial," Dice Machine, etc. Big money made by agents renting and selling these machines.

CHAS. T. MALEY NOVELTY CO., Cincinnati, O.

(1894)

KICK IF YOU DONT GET THE
GENERAL ARTHUR CIGAR
ON SALE ALL OVER THE UNITED STATES.
KERBS, WERTHEIM & SCHIFFER,
Manufacturers,
NEW YORK.
Send 2-cent Stamp for our Latest Cigar Folder.

(1894)

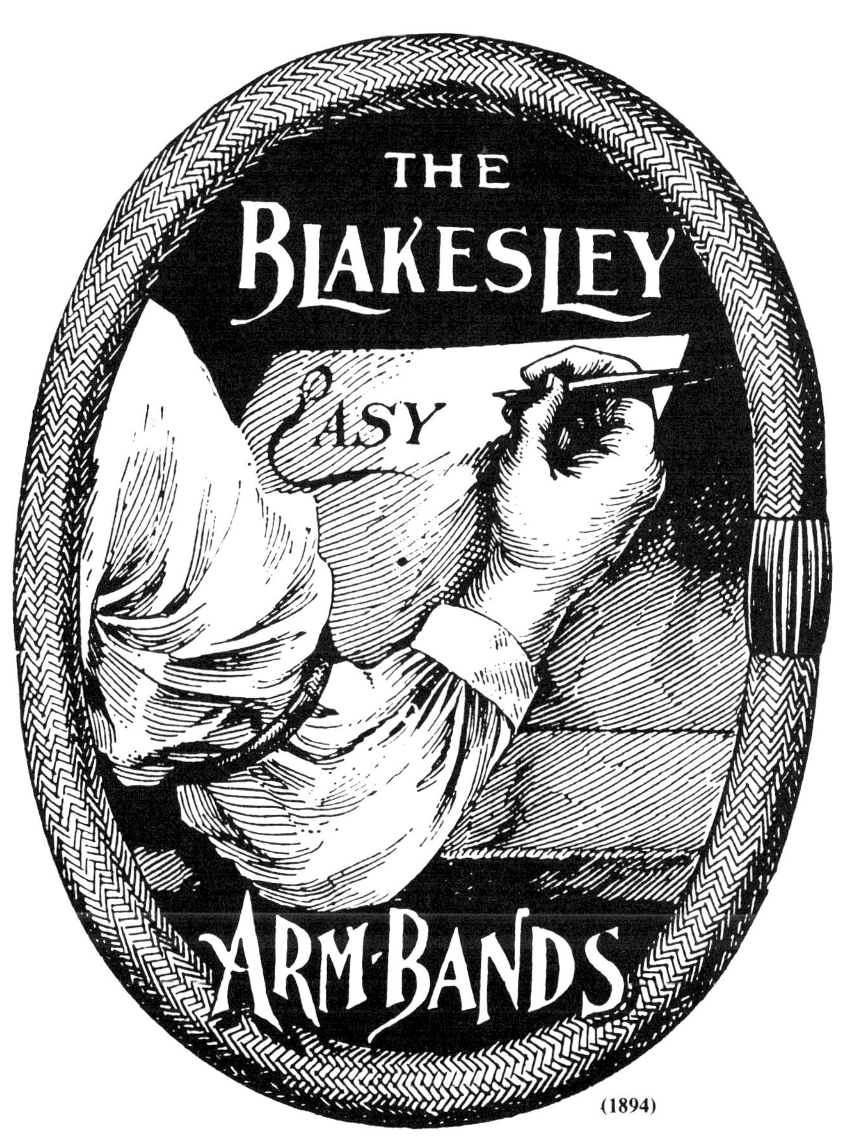

(1894)

"OUR COMBINATION."

KNEE-PANTS SUIT, EXTRA PAIR PANTS and HAT to Match, for Boys, ages 4 to 14 years. } ALL FOR **$5.00.**

BEST VALUE EVER OFFERED.

Strictly all wool. Best of styles. Perfect-fitting. Great variety. Single or double breasted. Sample pieces of the goods the "Combinations" are made from and rules for measuring sent free to any address. Clothes sent to your nearest Express office, C. O. D., with privilege of examining before paying. If they do not suit you they will be returned at our expense.

If you cannot wait to see samples, send age, weight and height of boy, and size of hat, and we will send the "Combination" and guarantee the fit. Or if money and 60 cents for postage is sent with the order, we will refund all the money if clothes do not fit and satisfy.

Our $15 Suits for Men, any style preferred, **best value in the world,** sent on same terms as above.

Finely Illustrated Spring Catalogue of Men's & Boys' Clothing and Furnishings sent free to any address.

PUTNAM CLOTHING HOUSE, Chicago, Ill.

(1894)

"No, thank you, Doctor, we don't need
you any more. We have all been cured
by the American Herbal Remedies."

(1895)

FOR
LADIES' AND CHILDREN'S BOOTS AND SHOES.

Awarded highest honors at

Philadelphia	1876	Melbourne	1880
Berlin	1877	Frankfort	1881
Paris	1878	Amsterdam	1883

And wherever else exhibited.

(1894)

Are easily and painlessly Filled at Home without previous experience by using **Dr. Hale's Home Dental Outfit** and method. It prevents toothache and early loss by stopping the cause, and secures *perfect, permanent teeth.* Every article in the outfit is warranted to be first-class. Money promptly refunded if unsatisfactory. Price, $3.00 and $5.00, with full directions, post-paid.

National Dental Supply Co.,
42 Warren St., Boston, Mass.

BUFFALO LITHIA WATER
Spring No. 2.
A SOLVENT FOR STONE IN THE BLADDER.

Dr. B. J. Weistling, *of Middletown, Pa., states:*

"Experience in its use in Stone in the Bladder, in my own person, enables me to attest the efficacy of the **BUFFALO LITHIA WATER** in this painful malady. After having been subjected to sufferings, the intensity of which cannot be described, I have, under the influence of the water, **passed an ounce of Calculi** (Uric Acid), **some of which weighed as much as four grains,** affording inexpressible relief and leaving me in a condition of comparative ease and comfort. **"On one occasion I passed thirty-five Calculi in forty-eight hours.** The appearance of this Calculus Nuclei indicates unmistakably, I think, that they were all component particles of one large Calculus, **destroyed by the action of the water, by means of solution and disintegration.** At my advanced period of life (I am seventy-seven years and six months of age), and in my feeble general health, a surgical operation was not to be thought of, and **the water seems to have accomplished all that such an operation, if successful, could have done."**

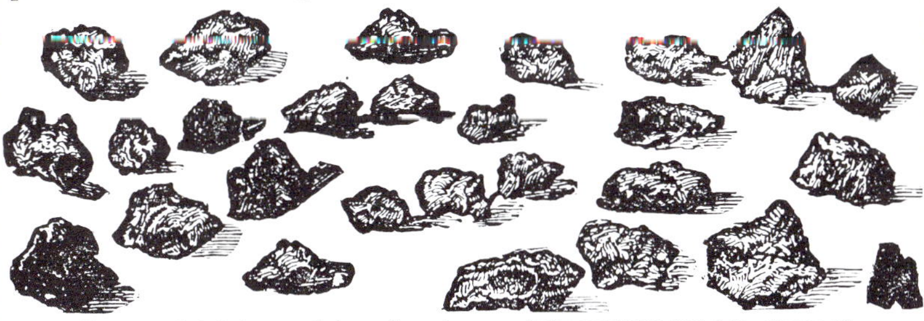

The above plate is from a photograph, and represents the exact size and shape of some of the Calculi passed by Dr. Weistling.

This Water is for sale by druggists generally, or in cases of one dozen half-gallon bottles $5.00 f.o.b. at the Springs. Descriptive pamphlets sent to any address.

THOMAS F. GOODE, Proprietor, Buffalo Lithia Springs, Va.

(1895)

Is what it is named.

It is **not** a signal to show that a bicycle is coming, but an **aid**, recognized by such riders as R. P. Searle, who says:—

Gentlemen: I have just finished my second record breaking trip from Chicago to New York. I used your lamp on all my night runs, sometimes running at a speed of fifteen miles per ho r in the dark. I was only able to make this fast time by the splendid light which I was enabled to obtain with the use of your lamp. I used your lamp because I considered it the best in the world to-day, and it has far exceeded my expectations. Yours, very truly,

R. P. SEARLE.

Points of Superiority Over every other Lantern made:

Central draft---burns 1o hours.
Burns kerosene oil unmixed.
Flame absolutely adjustable (by set screw.)
Filled and lighted from outside.

Saves Doctors' bills, barked shins, soiled clothing, and **makes riding** when there is the most leisure **a pleasure.**

Don't be insulted by having a cheap Lantern offered you which may possess possibly one characteristic, **but insist** *on having* the **Search Light,** which will be delivered free, if your dealer won't supply you, for the price, $5.00. Circular free. Address

BRIDGEPORT BRASS CO., Bridgeport, Conn.

(1895)

ARABIAN JOINT OIL.

A most wonderful discovery for producing a high degree of elasticity to the joints and muscles of the human body; it also removes aches and pains.

USED BY GYMNASTS AND ACROBATS.

Perfectly harmless, yet wonderfully effective. The only oil of the kind ever offered to the public. Price, $1.00; sample, 50 cts. Agents wanted. A liberal discount to the trade. Mention the Youth's Companion. Address

ARABIAN JOINT OIL CO., BOX 837, SPRINGFIELD, ILL.

(1887)

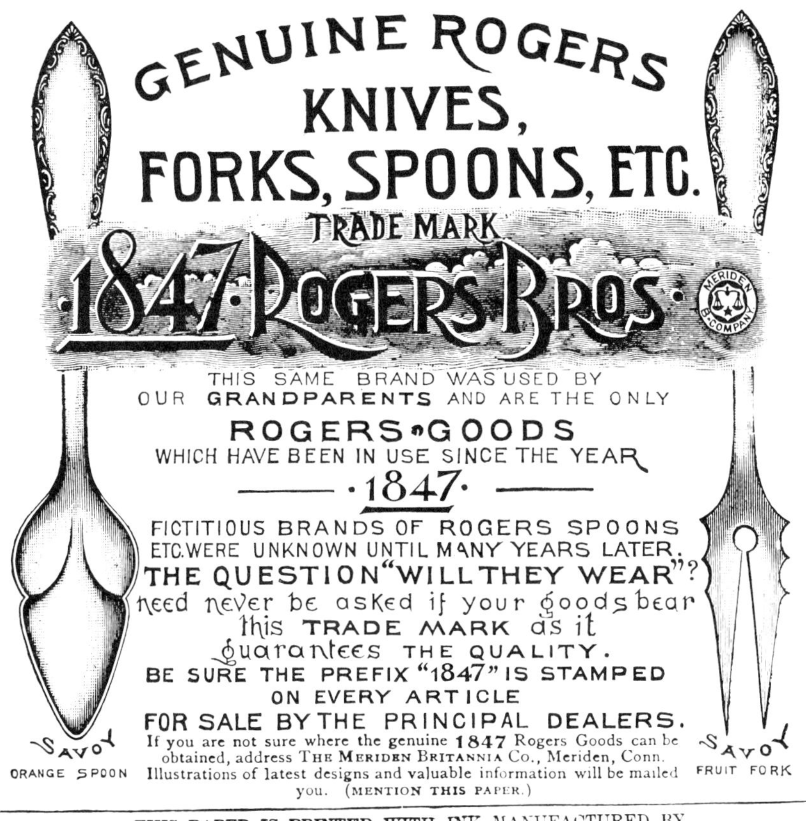

THIS PAPER IS PRINTED WITH INK MANUFACTURED BY

J. HARPER BONNELL CO.,

NEW YORK, CHICAGO.

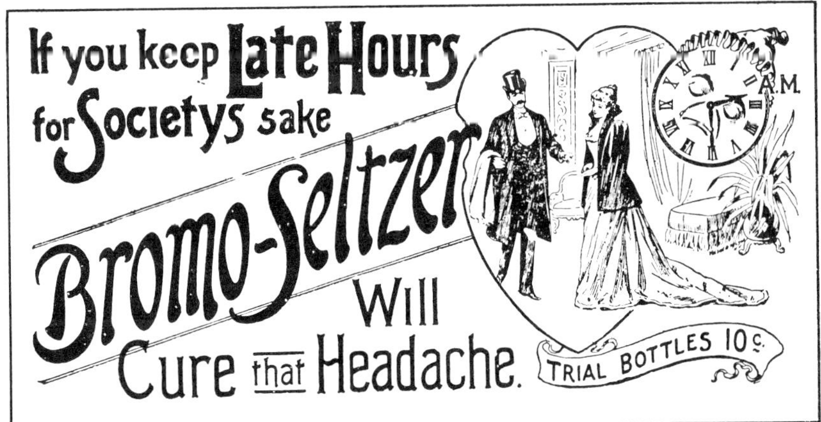

(1895)

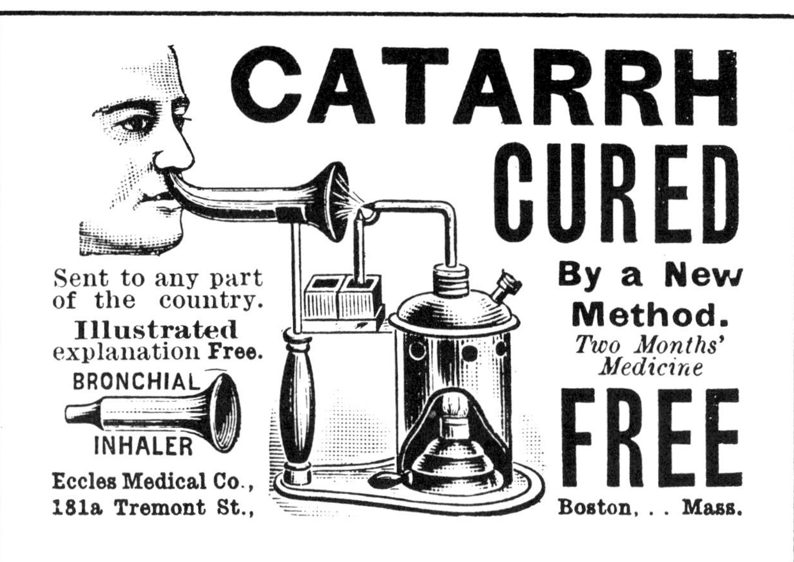

R. GREEN, M.D.-
INDIAN PHYSICIAN,
No. 38 BROMFIELD STREET,
BOSTON,

Has, with his INDIAN REMEDIES, treated with complete success more than 50,000 cases of CHRONIC DISEASES His practice is attended with complete triumph in cases of CANCER, SCROFULA, and all CHRONIC DISEASES.

The discovery of a plaster that will draw out CANCERS, with all their roots, without injury to the surrounding parts, and a remedy like the INDIAN PANACEA, which will cleanse the blood of all humors, are triumphs in medical science never before achieved.

His medicines are all VEGETABLE, and act in harmony with the laws of life; and so perfectly do they cleanse the blood of all disease, that out of several thousand cases of CANCER and SCROFULA which he has cured, not a case can be found where the disease has ever troubled them afterwards.

Consultations, personally or by letter, upon all diseases, free of charge. Circulars with full reference, sent by mail free.   1t   mar 24

THE MUSIC OF COMMERCE
SHOULD BE PLAYED ON THE
BEST INSTRUMENT
The
Columbia Bar-Lock
TYPEWRITER
FOR CATALOGUE & FULL PARTICULARS ADDRESS
COLUMBIA TYPEWRITER M'F'G Co
37 WEST 116TH STREET, NEW YORK.

(1895)

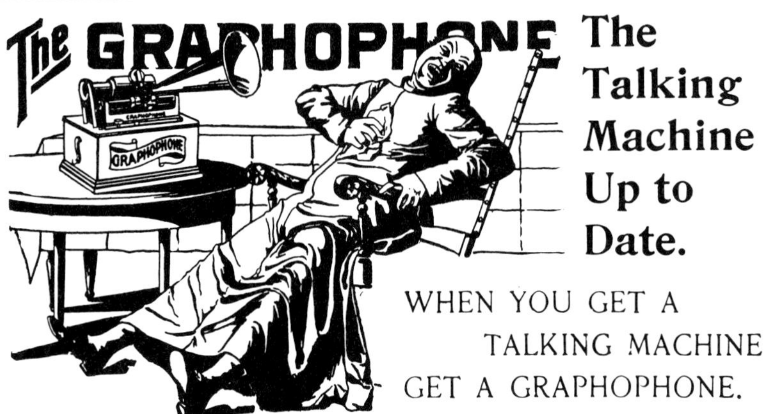

Why the Graphophone?

IN THE FIRST PLACE

The Graphophone reproduces perfectly and delightfully the music of bands, orchestras, and vocal and instrumental soloists. With a Graphophone one can provide at any time a most enjoyable entertainment, having the whole range of melody to draw on for his programme.

It is all musical instruments in one.

AND THEN

On a Graphophone cylinder any one can record easily and instantly music, the human voice, or any sound, and the record can be reproduced immediately and as often as desired. Only on talking machines manufactured under the Graphophone patents can sound be recorded, the performances of other so-called talking machines being limited to the reproduction of records of cut-and-dried subjects made in laboratories.

Graphophones are sold for $10 and up.

Write for Catalogue B. A.

COLUMBIA PHONOGRAPH CO., Dept. B. A.

NEW YORK, 143 and 145 Broadway.
RETAIL BRANCH, 1155–1157–1159 Broadway.
ST. LOUIS, 720–722 Olive St.
BALTIMORE, 110 E. Baltimore St.
BUFFALO, 313 Main St.

CHICAGO, 211 State St.
PARIS, 34 Boulevard des Italiens.
PHILADELPHIA, 1032 Chestnut St.
WASHINGTON, 919 Pennsylvania Ave
SAN FRANCISCO, 723 Market St.

(1898)

(1898)

My
O-Sage
Hair
Tonic
cleans your head of dandruff, makes your hair beautiful and
grows hair.   Sample postpaid, 5c.   Agents wanted.
DR. LYMAN, - - 615 Mill Street, Peoria, Ill.

(1910)

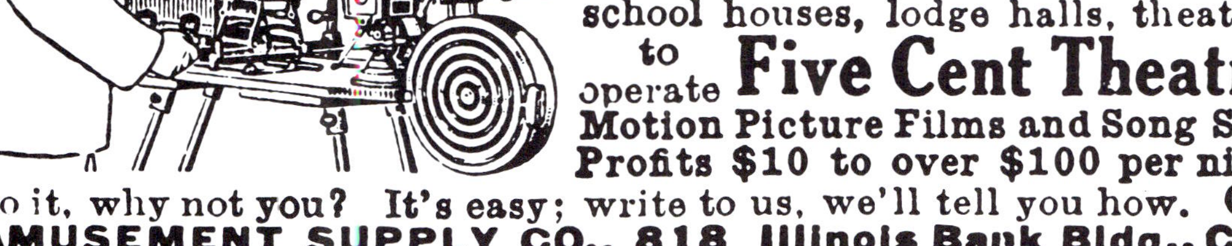

IT PAYS BIG
To Amuse The
Public With
Motion Pictures
NO EXPERIENCE NECESSARY as our instruction Book and "Business Guide" tells all. We furnish Complete Outfit with Big Advertising Posters, etc. Humorous dramas brimful of fun, travel, history, religion, temperance work and songs illustrated. One man can do it. Astonishing Opportunity in any locality for a man with a little money to show in churches, school houses, lodge halls, theaters, etc. and to operate Five Cent Theatres in store rooms. Motion Picture Films and Song Slides rented. Profits $10 to over $100 per night. Others do it, why not you? It's easy; write to us, we'll tell you how. Catalog free.
AMUSEMENT SUPPLY CO., 818 Illinois Bank Bldg., Chicago, Ill.

(1910)

(1899)

A BOTTLE OF THIS SHOULD BE IN EVERY HOME.

(1893)

The Men We Love
and
The Men We Marry

Are there generally two men in a woman's life — the man she loves and the man she marries?

A woman, keenly observant, and who has seen much of girls and women, holds that it is more often true than many suppose. Then she explains how it comes about: what it can mean, in suffering, to a woman, and what is the duty of a woman to be the wife of the man she married, not that of the man she wishes she had married.

A thoroughly feminine article is this. Men will not understand it, but women will.

It is in the October LADIES' HOME JOURNAL.

15 Cents Everywhere

(1910)

(1910)

154

Waterman's Ideal Fountain Pen

For Out-of-Doors Writing

The fountain pen you have used for years is also made in a style termed Waterman's Ideal Safety Pen. "Safety" principally because it is entirely safe for women to carry in hand-bag or trunk, in any position, as no ink can escape.

The Safety is well termed the "Out-Door-Pen" for, since it may be carried upside down or any way, it provides the only satisfactory pen which the women folk and children can carry around and use for their vacation writing.

The safety feature will also be especially appreciated by men when the vest is discarded for the Summer months, and this ready "Safety" takes its place in the trousers' pocket.

Golfers, autoists, boat people and all present-day lovers of out-of-door life will find Waterman's Ideal Safety Pen the greatest boon to their convenience that has ever been produced for writing.

Waterman's Ideal Safety Pen has all the superior qualities and writing advantages of the universal Waterman's Ideal, in addition to being so made that the cap screws over the ink barrel and corks it. Handsomely finished and strongly made. 14 kt. gold pen (all degrees). Will last for years.

Ask Your Dealer.   Avoid Substitutes.

L. E. Waterman Co., 173 Broadway, N. Y.

8 School St., Boston.   New No. 115 So. Clark St., Chicago.
17 Stockton St., San Francisco.   Kingsway, London.
6 Rue de Hanovre, Paris.
L. E. Waterman Company, Limited, Montreal.

(1911)

Every Reader of The Literary Digest can have a Roll of ScotTissue Towels at Absolutely no Cost to Himself

We want you to know of the advantages of the ScotTissue Towels right in your home and we are willing to buy a roll for you. Just write us, giving the name of the nearest druggist, and we will send you by return mail, an order or coupon, which will be redeemed by your druggist for a roll of ScotTissue towels, and a booklet telling of many uses.

This offer is only for readers of The Literary Digest and will not be made again— there are no strings to it—we want to get the roll of ScotTissue Towels in your home, and we take this method of doing it. The coupon is redeemed by us from the druggist at the full retail price of the towels, 35 cents. (50c West of Mississippi River).

ScotTissue Towels not only have the advantage of being hygienic and sanitary, but they are the greatest *convenience* in the home. In the kitchen they have a number of uses and advantages in addition to replacing the ordinary roller towel. They can be used for polishing cut glass; for absorbing surplus grease from fried foods; for wiping windows. Then, too, after shaving they dry the skin without friction, and eliminate the necessity for using powder.

Physicians and Dentists will immediately recognize the value of ScotTissue Towels in their own offices and homes; absolutely clean and sanitary, used once and thrown away, they eliminate the laundering necessary for the fabric towel.

Sit right down and write us for this coupon—then use the towels—and learn of the many uses for ScotTissue Towels both in the home and in public places.

Scott Paper Company

608 Glenwood Avenue   *Philadelphia, Pa.*

(1912)

Spice Develops the Flavor of Fruits

and other ingredients with which they are combined. When properly used, they give a subtle flavor that will convert a plain dessert into a tempting and unusual dish.

Stickney & Poor's Spices hold their strength longest. They retain their flavor and aroma because in the grinding process they are cut instead of crushed. They are weighed and packed automatically, so full weight and perfect cleanliness are insured.

Stickney & Poor's Products are: Mustard, Pepper, Cinnamon, Cloves, Ginger, Mace, Pimento, Sage, Savory, Marjoram, Celery, Salt, Curry Powder, Paprika, Tapioca, Nutmeg, Cassia, Allspice, Whole Mixed Spice, Pastry Spice, Turmeric, Thyme, Soda, Cream of Tartar, Rice Flour, Potato Flour, Sausage Seasoning, Poultry Seasoning and Flavoring Extracts.

Write for our book of receipts ; you will be delighted with it.

STICKNEY & POOR SPICE CO.
184 State St., Boston

 **THE NATIONAL**  
MUSTARD POT

(1913)

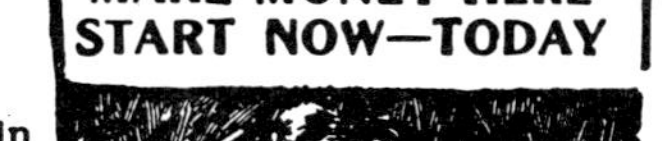

AGENTS
SALESMAN MANAGERS YOUNG OR OLD NEW BUSINESS

NEW BUSINESS JUST OUT

DROP THE DEAD ONES. AWAKE! START WITH THIS NEW INVENTION THE 20th CENTURY WONDER

Get started in an honest, clean, reliable, permanent, money-making business. Sold on a money-back guarantee

The Blackstone Water Power Vacuum Massage Machine

For the Home. No Cost to Operate. Lasts Life-Time

LISTEN No Competition, New Field, New Business. Price within reach of all. That's why it's easy to sell. Endorsed by Doctors and Masseurs. Removes Blackheads, Pimples, Wrinkles, rounds out any part of the face or body, brings back Nature's beauty. Almost instant relief can be given all kinds of pains such as Rheumatism, Headache, Backache, Neuralgia, and many times a permanent cure. A demonstration convinces the most skeptical person. Sales easily made.

Read On! What Others Do, So Can You.

Parker writes, sold eight machines first day. Margwarth says, I am making $19.00 per day. Schermerhorn, eight dozen machines first month. Shaffer writes, am selling four out of five demonstrations. Vaughn, orders one dozen, four days later wires "ship six dozen by first Express." Lewis, sells four first hour. Men, women, everybody makes money. No experience necessary. Protected territory to active workers. We own all patents. Big book entitled, "The Power and Love of Beauty and Health" Free. Investigate now, today. A postal will do. A big surprise awaits you. Address BLACKSTONE M'F'G CO., 725 Meredith Bldg., TOLEDO, OHIO

AGENTS
GENERAL AGENTS ROAD MEN MAKE MONEY HERE START NOW—TODAY

(1913)

To complete a good dinner a

Knox Gelatine Dessert

You will give your guests the right, delicious and satisfying morsel, when you serve one of the **KNOX GELATINE** desserts.   Try this for dinner—

Knox Spanish Cream

1 envelope **Knox** Sparkling Gelatine.

3 eggs.
1 quart milk.

1 tablespoonful vanilla.
8 tablespoonfuls sugar.

Soak gelatine in milk.   Put on fire and stir until dissolved.   Add yolks of eggs and 4 tablespoonfuls sugar well beaten.   Stir until it comes to the boiling point. Remove from stove and have whites of eggs well beaten with 4 tablespoonfuls sugar.   Add whites, stirring briskly until thoroughly mixed.   Flavor and turn into mold.   If desired, serve with whipped cream.   This will separate and form a jelly in the bottom with custard on top.

THE KNOX RECIPE BOOK

Contains choice recipes for Desserts, Salads, Candies. Jellies, Puddings, Ice Cream, Sherbets, etc. Sent FREE for your Grocer's name.   Pint sample for 2 cent stamp.

CHARLES B. KNOX CO., 7 Knox Ave., Johnstown, N.Y.

(1913)

Something New

TOTALLY, RADICALLY DIFFERENT

from any Sardines you ever tasted.

The Best of the Cleanest Fish That Swims:

cleaned, cooked, prepared with purest oils, spices, vinegar, etc , without preservatives or artificial coloring; packed in sanitary enamel-lined packages; thoroughly sterilized.

A DAINTY MORSEL YOU'LL FIND A TREAT.
A LUNCHEON NIBBLE THAT CAN'TBE BEAT.

Spreads like butter.
All Ready To Serve.
They're simply great.
10 and 15 cts. per package.
At dealers generally

EMERY & CO., INC.

Boston, Mass.

If not at your dealer's, 3 tins sent postpaid for 30cts.

(1913)

"Now for
SLADE'S PURE SALAD CREAM
SLADE'S
SALAD CREAM"
PLEASES THE PALATE,
arouses the appetite, assists digestion
and conduces to good health. Made
from the purest, freshest and most
wholesome ingredients. Free from oil,
artificial coloring and chemical preser-
vatives. Better than home-made dress-
ings and uniform in its excellence. Ask
Grocers for it. Free Booklet, "How to Make
Salads and Sandwiches," sent on request.
D. & L. SLADE CO., Boston.

(1913)

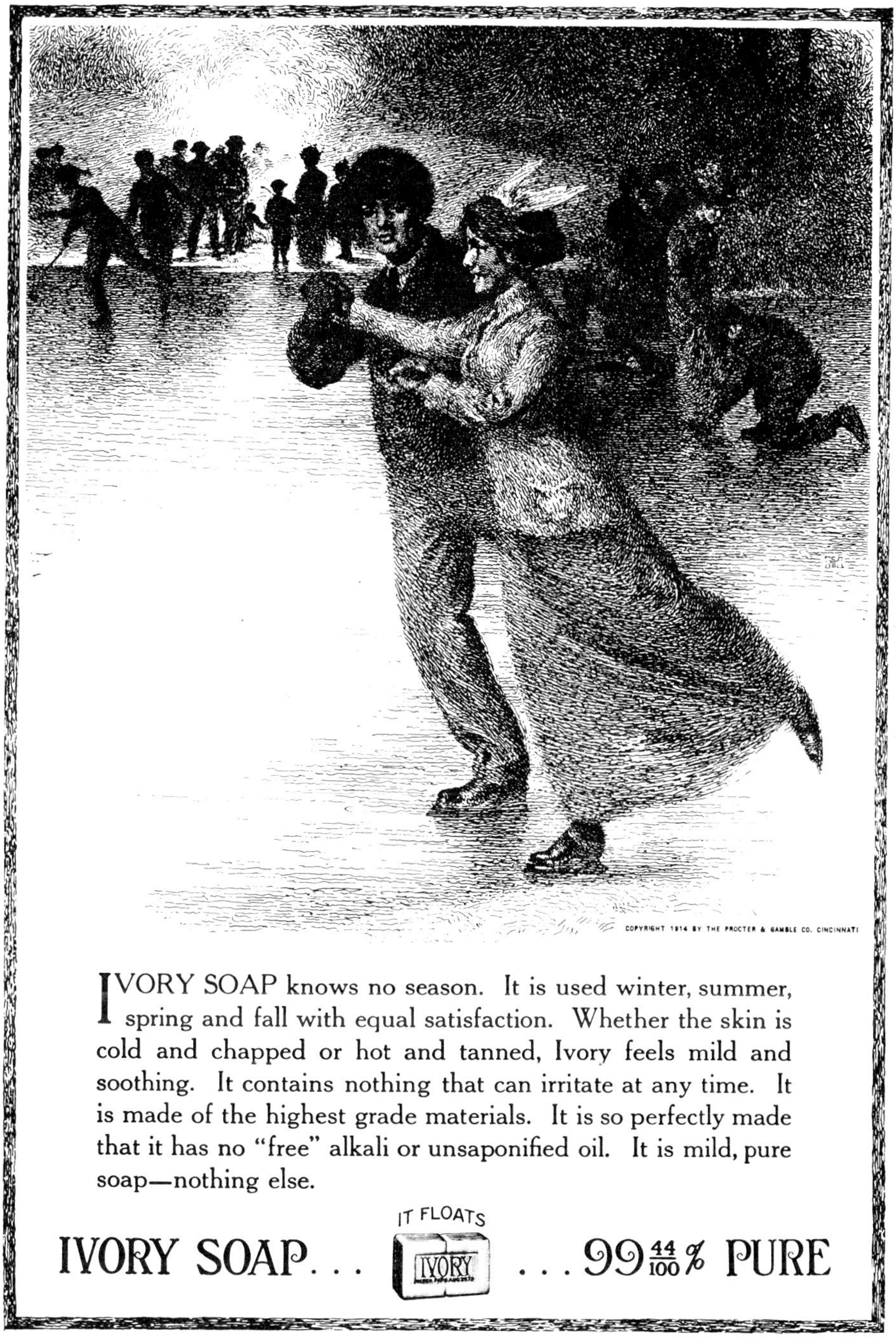

IVORY SOAP knows no season. It is used winter, summer, spring and fall with equal satisfaction. Whether the skin is cold and chapped or hot and tanned, Ivory feels mild and soothing. It contains nothing that can irritate at any time. It is made of the highest grade materials. It is so perfectly made that it has no "free" alkali or unsaponified oil. It is mild, pure soap—nothing else.

IVORY SOAP... IT FLOATS ...99 44/100 % PURE

(1914)

The Entire Family Will Like Holstein Cows' Milk

It is a well "balanced" milk without the predominance of butter fat. This predominance of butter fat occurs in the milk of those cows whose development has been due to a desire for abnormal butter fat producers. The fat globules in Holstein Cows' Milk are smaller and therefore more easily absorbed when taken as food. This fineness of fat is also noted in mothers' milk, for which Holstein Cows' Milk is the best substitute.

The same properties which make Holstein Cows' Milk baby food recommend it for general home consumption. It is naturally a light colored milk, containing more of the protein, and the fat it contains is more finely emulsified.

Holstein Cows' Milk is valuable for lunch — it is a food. A glass of it between meals is satisfying and refreshing. As an ingredient in all recipes that require milk it possesses distinct advantages.

You should know more about the milk of this black-and-white cow. May we send our booklet, "The Story of Holstein Milk?"

HOLSTEIN-FRESIAN ASSOCIATION
4-W American Building   **Brattleboro, Vermont**

(1915)

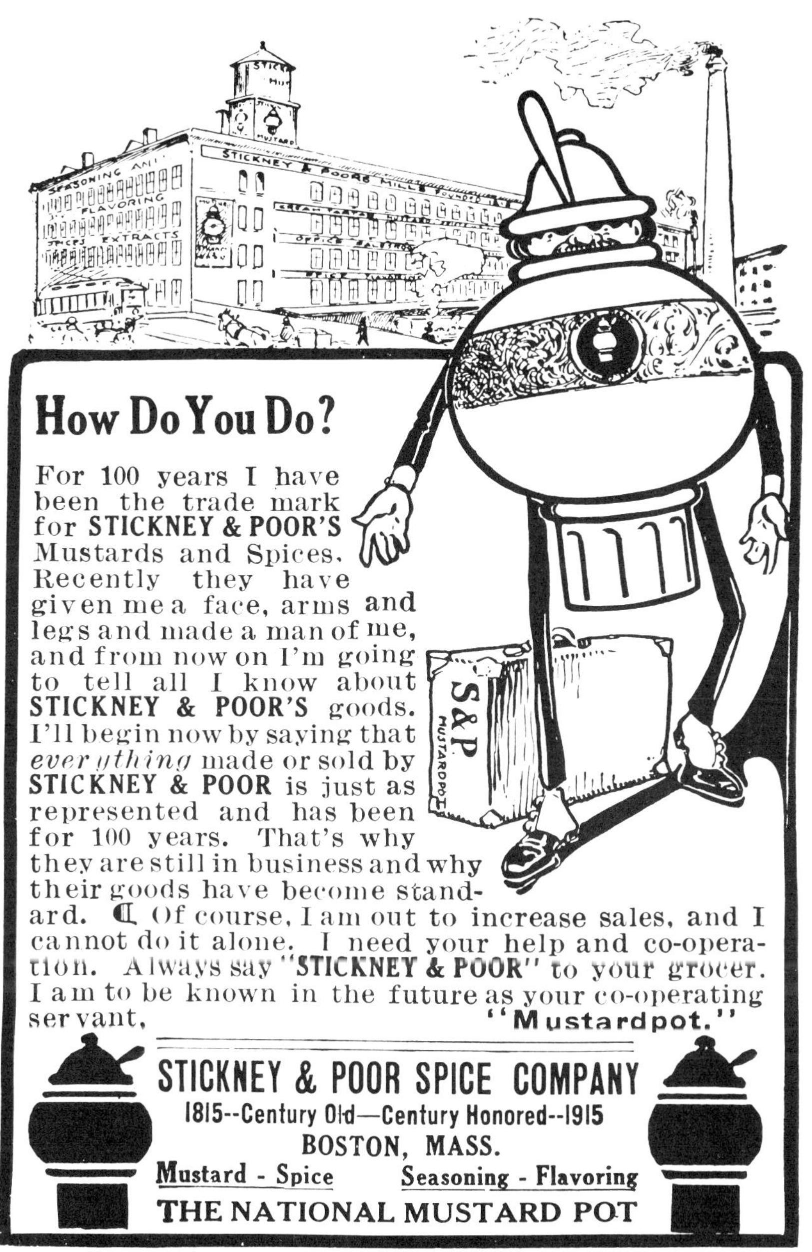
How Do You Do?
For 100 years I have been the trade mark for STICKNEY & POOR'S Mustards and Spices. Recently they have given me a face, arms and legs and made a man of me, and from now on I'm going to tell all I know about STICKNEY & POOR'S goods. I'll begin now by saying that everything made or sold by STICKNEY & POOR is just as represented and has been for 100 years. That's why they are still in business and why their goods have become standard. Of course, I am out to increase sales, and I cannot do it alone. I need your help and co-operation. Always say "STICKNEY & POOR" to your grocer. I am to be known in the future as your co-operating servant, "Mustardpot."
S&P MUSTARDPOT
STICKNEY & POOR SPICE COMPANY
1815--Century Old—Century Honored--1915
BOSTON, MASS.
Mustard - Spice   Seasoning - Flavoring
THE NATIONAL MUSTARD POT

(1915)

RAE'S LUCCA OIL

"The Perfection of Olive Oil."

Guaranteed to be "THE VERY FINEST PURE OLIVE OIL" for eating purposes produced.

SOLD IN BOTTLES AND TINS OF VARIOUS SIZES

S. RAE & CO.
LEGHORN, ITALY

(1915)

(1915)

The Dessert
Question Answered-

Your well planned dinner will be largely judged by the last impression. A dessert made of Sea Moss Farine is always pleasing and satisfying to particular people. Try these recipes by the renowned Madame Gesine Lemcke.

Delicious Blanc Mange
Tasty and Wholesome.

Put one cupful sugar in a double boiler, add two teaspoonfuls Sea Moss Farine, mix together, add one quart milk, a sprinkle of salt, cover and cook ten minutes, stirring occasionally. Flavor to suit with two teaspoonfuls vanilla or other flavor. Pour into 6 or 8 cups, previously rinsed with cold water. Serve ice cold with fruit sauce or cream or Blanc Mange can be poured into a form.

Toothsome Puddings
quickly and easily prepared.

Snow Pudding.—Mix two teaspoonfuls Sea Moss Farine with ¾ cupful sugar, add one quart cold milk, the thin peel of one lemon a sprinkle of salt, cover and cook ten minutes; flavor with 1 teaspoonful almond extract, remove lemon peel, beat the whites of 4 eggs to a stiff froth, add the hot Farine whilst beating constantly, rinse a form with cold water, pour in the mixture and set on ice. Serve with fruit or vanilla sauce.

Sea Moss Farine

Strictly a Vegetable Product Prepared from Genuine Sea Moss.

Price 25 cents per package, enough for a family's daily desserts for one month.

AT ALL GROCERS OR SENT BY MAIL POSTPAID.

**Send for Sample and
Mrs. Lemcke's Recipe Book, Free.**

**LYON MANUFACTURING CO.,
38 South Fifth St.,   Brooklyn, N. Y.** (1915)

DOWN HIGH COST LIVING

REVERE
Baking Powder

¼ pound   5c

½ pound 10c

1 pound 20c

5 pounds 75c

PURE—WHOLESOME
Efficient — Economical

Ask Grocers for REVERE

D. & L. SLADE CO., Boston

(1915)

To convince you

that you can make a truly remark-able improvement in the aroma, flavor and color of your soups, gravies and sauces, by using

Kitchen Bouquet

(Reg. U. S. Pat. Off.)

we want to send you a

FREE SAMPLE BOTTLE

with our book of tested recipes. Send for it now. You will save time, trouble and get results in cooking you have never gotten before. Name your grocer and send today.

THE PALISADE MFG. CO.
353 Clinton Ave., West Hoboken, N. J.

(1915)

Henderson Certified
Automatic Chainstitch

HENDERSON AUTOMATIC

CERTIFIED
SERVICE

A Sewing Machine with four drawers automatic lift chain
of steel "Certified for 10 years." And will last your life
time. Complete with all accessories.

Others charge $75 to $80—Our price $45

30 DAYS FREE TRIAL

Send your name and references

WE DELIVER FREE. And if you are pleased at the end
of 30 days, pay us for machine. If not, we cheerfully
withdraw the machine at our expense.

F. C. HENDERSON CO. MANUFACTURERS
DISTRIBUTORS

480 Washington Street, Boston, Mass.

(1915)

ICY-HOT BOTTLE
FREE

For 19 coupons (8 mill value) taken from cans of Alexander's products and this "ad" (which has 3 mill value) or coupons totaling 60 mills, will send our No. 8 Icy-Hot Bottle. Offer made to stimulate growing demand for Alexander's Pure Foods.

ALEXANDER'S
DOVE BRAND
NEW ORLEANS
MOLASSES

For Gingerbread, Boston Brown Bread, Home-made Candies. Has the real old-fashioned plantation flavor. Two grades:

Blue Label (Golden Color)
White Label (Better Quality)
Ask Grocer to order today
ALEXANDER MOLASSES COMPANY
CINCINNATI
A'exander's Fancy Cane Syrup
for Griddle Cakes

The DOVE BRAND
REFINED NEW ORLEANS
MOLASSES

(1915)

An Ounce or a Pound?

The world has long since concluded that "an ounce of prevention is worth a pound of cure." Those who render a real service to humanity—are those who conserve health.

Pure, wholesome food is a well-known preventive of ill-health; and for twenty-five years **Calumet Baking Powder** has excelled as a preparer of good food.

People who have investigated the action, properties and residue of various leavening agents, recommend "**CALUMET.**" The ingredients used have been approved by the Remsen Board, appointed by the United States Government and composed of men whose ability is acknowledged.

A copy of the U. S. Bulletin, No. 103, containing the findings of the Remsen Board, will be sent upon request.

CALUMET BAKING POWDER CO., Chicago, Ill.

CALUMET
BAKING POWDER

(1916)

New Low Prices On Refrigerators

White Enameled—Steel Lined

Wonderful value at a low price, due to Montgomery Ward's enormous purchasing capacity.

Fine hardwood case — round corners — golden oak finish. Chamber lined with white enameled steel. Perfect insulation insuring ice saving. Easy to clean, as shelves, drain pipe and trap all are removable. Would cost $12 if bought in ordinary way. Send for regular Refrigerator circular and *save your money.*

New York   Chicago
Kansas City   Ft. Worth   *Montgomery Ward & Co.*   Dept. A D 497
Portland, Ore.

Address House Most Convenient

(1916)

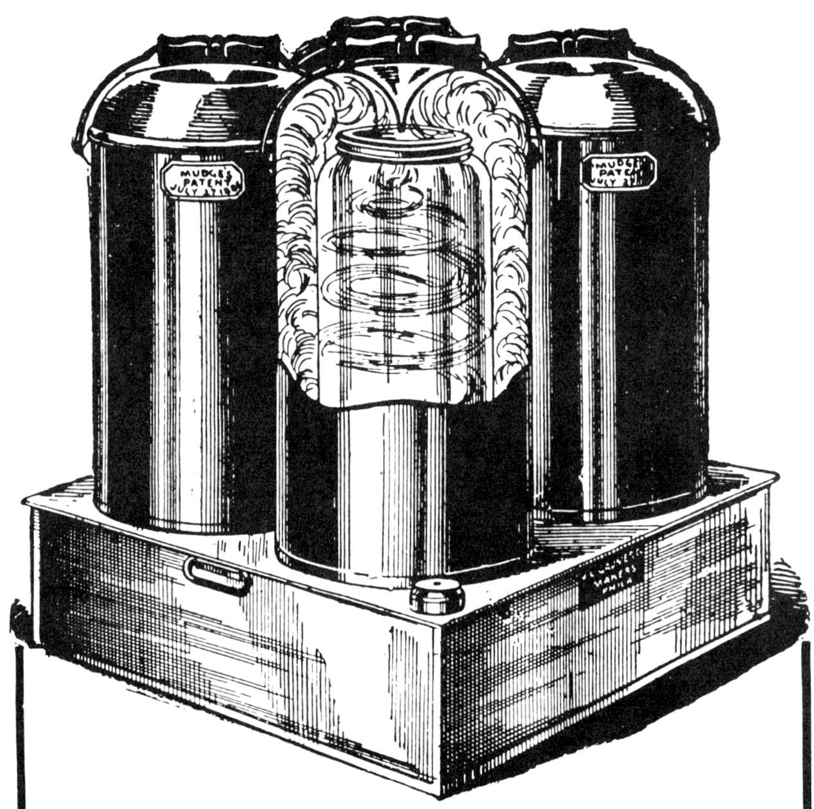

Mudge Patent Canner

The modern way of canning fruits and vegetables

A HOUSEHOLD NECESSITY

Write for information

BIDDLE-GAUMER COMPANY
3846-56 Lancaster Avenue,   Philadelphia, Pa.

(1916)

This Pastry Flour is very economical for quick biscuit, cake, pie-crust, short-cake, etc. Quality always uniform

December 2, 1915.

My daughter, being in the dramatic profession, is often obliged to travel, necessitating light housekeeping. At present, we are located in Boston.

Recently when playing in Portland, Me., I bought at a local store, some "White Puff" Flour. It was delicious, and I found it a great saving, because I only had to use half the shortening that I had used with other flours.

Now, really I want some more of this "White Puff" Flour as soon as possible, and will appreciate it very much if you notify me where I can buy it in Brookline.

I don't see how any good cook can get along without "White Puff". We certainly can't.

Yours truly,

MRS. F. H. CUSHMAN.

11 Devotion St.,
Brookline, Mass.

GET IT OF YOUR GROCER. IF HE DOES NOT
KEEP IT, WE WILL SUPPLY YOU DIRECT

WILLIAM S. HILLS CO., Boston

(1916)

178

Bowlegged Men

Your legs will appear straight when you wear

Straightleg Garters

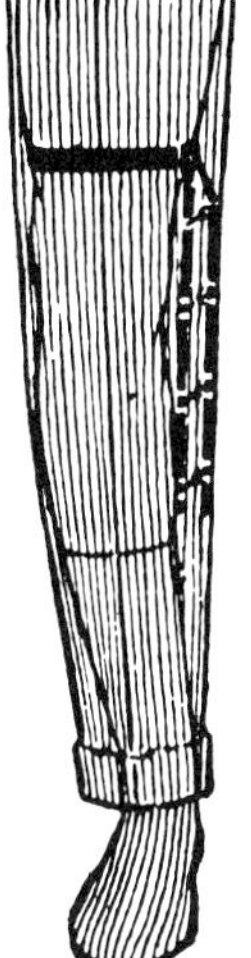

Remarkable brand-new invention—Combination hose-supporter and pantleg straightener—**Quickly adjusted to fit various degrees of bowlegs;** as easy to put on and comfortable to wear as any ordinary garter—**no harness or padded forms;** just an ingenious special garter for bowlegged men—improves appearance wonderfully. Write for free booklet, mailed in plain envelope.

S-L Garter Co.
618 City National Bank Bldg.
Dayton, Ohio

(1918)

STUDY
Journalism
AT HOME.

Reporting, Editing, all branches of newspaper and literary work taught

BY MAIL.
Practical work from the start. Improved methods. Best results.

The Sprague Correspondence School of Journalism.

Catalogue FREE.
No. 2 Telephone Bldg.
DETROIT, MICH.

(1895)

CAR OWNERS WANTED!
To use and introduce the great-est improvement in Inner Tubes since autos were invented. Air gauge in valve stem of every Tube shows at a glance through the Un-breakable Transparent Valve Cover amount of air in tires.
AIR-GAGE Heavy Duty Tubes
—sell on sight to almost every car owner because they save trouble, time, worry and expense. Add one-third to life of Tires. Paul salesmen make big profits selling direct to car owners. Our million dollar factory can use 500 more salesmen at once. Experience not necessary. Big illustrated Free Book tells how the Paul Plan will start you in this big money-making business without capital. Write for Free Book Today.
THE PAUL RUBBER CO.   Dept. 53
Salisbury, N. C.
(1)

(1923)

The Little Brown Jug
Old E. L. ANDERSON
Rye OR Bourbon
QUALITY UNSURPASSED.
Delivered in sealed case (no marks) at your home, Direct from the Dis-tillery. Save all middlemen's profits and adulterations. Buy of us at $2.90 per gallon. Write us for prices and full information. All busi-ness strictly confidential. Address
THE E. L. ANDERSON DISTILLING CO.,
Box No. 1500.   Newport, Kentucky.
THE FAMOUS OLD E.L.ANDERSON
PURE WHISKEY

(1894)

HAVE YOU A SWEETHEART,

Son or Brother in training camps in the American Army or Navy? If so, mail him a package of **ALLEN'S FOOT=EASE**, the antiseptic powder to be shaken into the shoes and sprinkled in the foot-bath. The American, British and French troops use Allen's Foot=Ease, because it takes the Friction from the Shoe and freshens the feet. It is the greatest comforter for tired, aching, tender, swollen feet, and gives relief to corns and bunions.

The Plattsburg Camp Manual advises men in training to shake Foot=Ease in their shoes each morning. Ask your dealer to-day for a 25c. box of Allen's Foot=Ease, and for a 2c. stamp he will mail it for you. What remembrance could be so acceptable?

(1918)

MEN GO WILD

about splendid teeth. Therefore, fair ladies, it behooves you to know that **Sozodont** makes them glitter like Orient pearls. By this pure Vegetable Dentifrice the enamel is rendered impervious to decay, all discolorations are removed, the gums become hard and rosy, and the *breath* is rendered pure and sweet. No lady ever used **Sozodont** without approving of its cleansing and purifying properties, and the flattering testimonials that have been bestowed upon it by eminent Dentists and scientific men, speak volumes of praise for its merits. **Sozodont** contains not one particle of acid or any ingredient whatever that will injure the enamel, and is free from the acrid properties of Tooth Pastes, etc. One bottle **Sozodont** will last six months.

(1898)

KENNEDY BROTHERS,
STAPLE & FANCY GROCERIES, FLOUR, FEED & SHIP STORES,
WINES, LIQUORS AND CIGARS,
23 UNION STREET, - - MIDDLETOWN, CONN.

W. L. DOUGLAS
$3 SHOE FOR GENTLEMEN.

$5.00 **Genuine Hand-sewed,** an elegant and stylish dress Shoe which commends itself.

$4.00 **Hand-sewed Welt.** A fine calf Shoe unequalled for style and durability.

$3.50 **Goodyear Welt** is the standard dress Shoe, at a popular price.

$3.50 **Policeman's Shoe** is especially adapted for railroad men, farmers, etc. All made in Congress, Button and Lace.

$3.00 **for Ladies,** is the only **hand-sewed** shoe sold at this popular price.

$2.50 **Dongola Shoe for Ladies,** is a new departure and promises to become very popular.

$2.00 **Shoe for Ladies, and $1.75 for Misses** still retain their excellence for style, etc.

All goods warranted and stamped with name on bottom. If advertised local agent cannot supply you, send direct to factory enclosing advertised price or a postal for order *111** blanks. **W. L. DOUGLAS, Brockton, Mass.**